Essential

KELVINGROVE

Key to symbols

Interactive area		Lift	
Female toilets		Accessible lift	
Male toilets		Shop	
Accessible toilets		Café	
Letterbox		Cloakroom	
Public telephone			

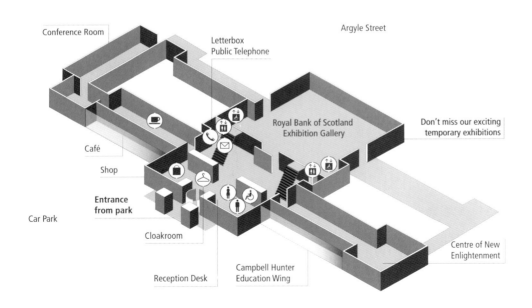

LOWER GROUND FLOOR

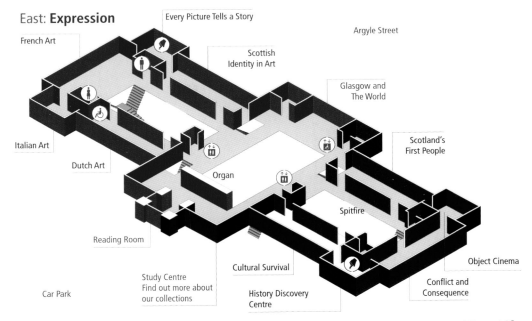

East: **Expression**

French Art

Every Picture Tells a Story

Scottish Identity in Art

Argyle Street

Glasgow and The World

Italian Art

Dutch Art

Organ

Scotland's First People

Reading Room

Spitfire

Scotland's First People

Object Cinema

Car Park

Study Centre Find out more about our collections

Cultural Survival

History Discovery Centre

Conflict and Consequence

FIRST FLOOR

West: **Life**

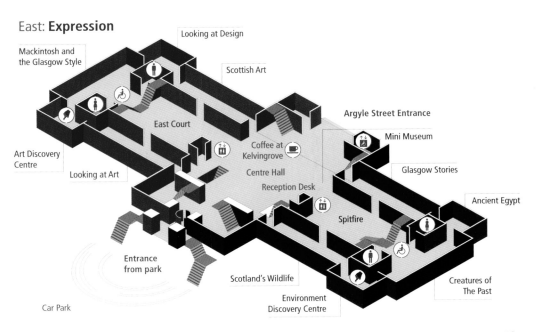

East: **Expression**

Looking at Design

Mackintosh and the Glasgow Style

Scottish Art

Argyle Street Entrance

Mini Museum

East Court

Coffee at Kelvingrove

Art Discovery Centre

Glasgow Stories

Looking at Art

Centre Hall

Reception Desk

Ancient Egypt

Spitfire

Entrance from park

Scotland's Wildlife

Car Park

Environment Discovery Centre

Creatures of The Past

GROUND FLOOR

West: **Life**

Essential
KELVINGROVE

Glasgow Museums Publishing in association with Philip Wilson Publishers

First published in 2010 by
Culture and Sport Glasgow (Museums)
in association with Philip Wilson Publishers

Philip Wilson Publishers
109 Drysdale Street
The Timber Yard
London N1 6ND

www.philip-wilson.co.uk

Distributed throughout the world (excluding North America) by
I.B. Tauris & Co. Ltd
6 Salem Road, London W2 4BU

Distributed in North America by
Palgrave Macmillan, a division of St Martin's Press
175 Fifth Avenue, New York NY 10010

ISBN 978-0-85667-691-8

Edited by Fiona MacLeod

This book is an abridged version of *Kelvingrove Art Gallery and
Museum: A souvenir guide*, published by Glasgow Museums
Publishing and Philip Wilson Publishers in 2009.

Editor for Philip Wilson Publishers: David Hawkins

Designed by Caroline and Roger Hillier
The Old Chapel Graphic Design
www.theoldchapelivinghoe.com

Photography supplied by Glasgow Museums
Photographers and Photo Library,
www.glasgowmuseums.com/photolibrary

Printed and bound in China by Everbest

Acknowledgements

All efforts have been made to trace copyright holders but if any have been
inadvertently omitted, please notify the publishers. The publishers gratefully
acknowledge the following for permission to reproduce illustrations:

THE BRITISH MUSEUM Partnership UK Trustees of the British Museum, for permission to reproduce images of
the coffin and mummy of Ankhesnefer

John Byrne, *Self Portrait in Stetson* © John Byrne/Bridgeman Art

Joan Eardley, *Two Children* and *Glasgow Kids* © with permission of the Eardley
Estate

Marianne Grant, *Children Playing in the Ashes*, by kind permission of
Susan Slater and family

Margaret Hutchison collection, by kind permission of the donor

Mathias Kauage, *Buka War*, courtesy of Rebecca Hossack Art Gallery,
London, on behalf of Mathias Kauage

Sir John Lavery, *Anna Pavlova* © The Estate of Sir John Lavery by courtesy of
Felix Rosenstiel's Widow & Son Ltd., London

L.S. Lowry, *VE Day*, © The Estate of L.S. Lowry, 2008

Avril Paton ®, *Windows in the West* ®, by kind permission of the artist

Benno Schotz, *Ura* and *Self-Portrait*, permission granted by the Trustees of the
late Benno Schotz

The Singh Twins, *Mr Singh's India*, by kind permission of the artists,
image copyright The Singh Twins (www.singhtwins.co.uk)

As with all other museums and galleries, sometimes objects are on loan,
displayed in other venues, being conserved, or are co-owned, so we cannot
guarantee that every object in this book will be on display when you visit. If you
are interested in finding out more about any of Glasgow's collections, you can
visit the Kelvingrove Study Centre (behind the organ) or Glasgow Museums
Resource Centre or search our Collections Navigator:
http://collections.glasgowmuseums.com

Contents

Welcome to Kelvingrove

Paintings were hung so they could be enjoyed by all visitors

Kelvingrove is at once typical and unique. It is a typical Victorian museum founded by the wealthy classes to assert their cultural worth and to improve their city's citizens; it is also typical in its aspiration to create an encyclopaedia of global knowledge as expressed in real objects. What is unusual – possibly unique – about Kelvingrove is that its world-class collections and vast imposing building do not make it the special preserve of a narrow group of local residents. The majority of the citizens of Glasgow know that they own Kelvingrove, that it is *their* museum.

The 2003–6 redisplay of Kelvingrove was built on Victorian traditions and ideals, but updated for the twenty-first century. The impossible ideal of a complete encyclopaedia was changed to tell the most interesting stories about the most interesting objects in the collections. Each gallery is a themed gathering of these stories, reflecting the variety of life and the range of human experience. The response of the public has been overwhelmingly positive – 3.2 million visits were made in the first year after reopening. *The Observer*'s reviewer concluded that the new Kelvingrove is 'Not so much a museum of culture as of life itself ... part National Gallery, part V&A, part British Museum and Tate – all in one building.'

Mark O'Neill
Head of Arts and Museums
Culture and Sport Glasgow

Kelvingrove's Life Court

Kelvingrove Art Gallery and Museum

Kelvingrove Art Gallery and Museum was built expressly to house the collections owned by the City of Glasgow. A special committee was formed to organize the huge International Exhibition in Kelvingrove Park in 1888 with the ambitious aim of raising the funds to build a new museum worthy of their

Kelvingrove (centre) with the 1901 International Exhibition building next door

city. They succeeded, although it took 13 years to complete the project, at a cost of £250,000.

When the Duchess of Fife opened Kelvingrove on 2 May 1901, it was as the centrepiece of an even more splendid international exhibition, held in Kelvingrove Park to celebrate the completion of the museum.

However the 'real' opening of the new Kelvingrove Art Gallery and Museum, housing the City's own collections, took place on 25 October 1902. On that day then Lord Provost Sir Samuel Chisholm described it memorably as 'a palace of dreams'.

People's memories of Kelvingrove are many and varied. Family visits on Sunday afternoons, the art competition and courting figure highly. Many are stirred by favourite objects from a hugely varied collection – Sir Roger the Elephant, the Dalí, the dinosaurs, Impressionist paintings, the beehive, the *Motherless* sculpture. The Kelvingrove experience is hard to define as it is so personal, but it seems to revolve around familiarity, a sense of pride that 'this belongs to us' and that somehow it always remains the same.

Hugh Stevenson
Curator, British Art

The great and the good at the 1901 opening

SCOTTISH ART

Some of the most innovative works of art ever painted in Scotland are on display in this gallery, and were created by two distinctive groups of Scottish artists between 1880 and 1930.

The Glasgow Boys revolutionized Scottish painting from 1880 until about 1895. Rebelling against traditional Victorian sentimentality, they painted everyday subjects in a fresh new way, often painting out of doors. The Scottish Colourists – Fergusson, Peploe, Cadell and Hunter – brought a colourful French style to Scottish painting from about 1900 until 1930. They all painted in a free and vigorous manner, using bright colours and with little attention to detail. Their style was influenced by the work of French artists such as Cézanne, Matisse and Derain.

The Druids — Bringing in the mistletoe 1890
George Henry
(1858–1943) and
Edward Atkinson Hornel
(1864–1933)
Oil on canvas
1524 x 1524 mm
Bought by Glasgow
Museums, 1922
1534

This is the most significant, unusual and forward-looking of all of the paintings by the Glasgow Boys, and was painted by two artists who were close friends. In subject and in the pattern of the frame we see a fascination for ancient Celtic art and folklore. The horns of the cattle are decorated with mistletoe, a plant revered by the Celtic priests for its magical and medicinal qualities. The high horizon line and the strongly triangular shape of the processional group give the picture a sense of immediacy. This, and the use of gold leaf, were revolutionary features for the time.

Old Willie — The village worthy 1886
James Guthrie
(1859–1930)
Oil on canvas
608 x 508 mm
Bought by Glasgow
Museums, 1974
3314

This is one of the finest portraits ever painted by any of the Glasgow Boys. Guthrie gives us a very honest and realistic picture of old Willie, faithfully depicting the lines on Willie's weather-beaten face and his ordinary clothes, and setting him simply against a whitewashed wall. All the compositional elements, including the clear light and clean colours, reflect the straightforward attitude and quiet dignity of the sitter's personality. Guthrie painted this work in Kirkcudbright, in Dumfries and Galloway. Several of the Glasgow Boys joined him there, finding their subjects in the surrounding scenery and the local people going about everyday tasks.

Anna Pavlova
1910
John Lavery
(1856–1941)
Oil on canvas
1981 x 1448 mm
Given by Nicol P.
Brown 1924
1581

In this exuberant picture of the Russian prima ballerina, Lavery aimed to capture the abandon and wild frenzied nature of the 'pas de deux' from Pepita's ballet *The Seasons*. This had caused a sensation when Pavlova performed it at her opening night at the Palace Theatre, London, in 1910. Although the dancer came to the artist's studio to pose over a three-month period, Lavery depicts her as if she is on stage. Her head is thrown back with her face in the shadows, while the theatrical lighting dramatically illuminates the rest of her body.

Interior — The Orange Blind c.1927
Francis Campbell Boileau Cadell
(1883–1937)
Oil on canvas
1118 x 864 mm
Given by the Trustees of the Hamilton Bequest, 1928
1763

Cadell's masterpiece, this picture positively oozes period charm. In typically Colourist style, the orange blind in the background provides the composition with a dazzling focal point and contrasts starkly with the bold expanses of black and green. Who is this mysterious lady taking tea, and who is the man playing the piano? We are left to ponder their identities and to admire the relaxed elegance and sophistication of a bygone era — all part of the picture's visual seduction. Cadell delights in the complicated arrangement of furniture and architectural features, which add to the picture's sense of nervous energy and expectation.

LOOKING AT DESIGN

In this gallery, we see that design matters because it shapes the world in which we live, and that designers' ideas and creativity can make a positive contribution to – or detract from – the quality of all our lives. Successful design understands how something will function and how we, the users, will interact with the design; it understands that appearance and aesthetics are important. Find out how the best design work welcomes us all as users, no matter how we differ from one another, and how responsible modern design uses the latest engineering and technological innovation while aiming to minimize its impact on the environment.

Polonaise gown c.1780–81
Brocaded silk, linen
1070 x 450 x 1200 mm
Given by Mrs Anne D. Houston,
1932
1932.51.l–m

The ties at the back of this gown pull the skirt up into three puffs, known as a 'polonaise'. The term is named after Poland, which was subdivided into three by Russia, Prussia and Austria in 1772. Mary, daughter of William Macdowall, of Castle Semple, wore this dress. She married George Houston of Johnstone Castle on 1 February 1779. They had two sons – Ludovic, born on 10 May 1780, and William, born on 18 September 1781. The large size of the bodice suggests that Mary may have worn this dress during the late stages of either pregnancy.

**Model of George
Bennie's Railplane** 1930s
305 x 965 mm
T.1931.5

This is a model of the George Bennie Railplane, an innovative idea for mass transit from the 1930s. Bennie was an inventor who wanted to revolutionize rail travel by separating passenger and freight traffic. This did not involve a new railway network, but a new style of propulsion.

Bennie proposed a carriage suspended from a rail above existing train lines. Powered by propeller engines and inspired by design techniques of the aircraft industry, this would transport passengers in a swift, sure, and safe fashion. Bennie built a test track near Milngavie, Glasgow, to show off his proposal, and there was interest in building Bennie Railplanes from both Britain and abroad. Unfortunately, the invention was not taken up commercially, and Bennie's idea of a railplane never materialized.

Anderson Special Mark II Motor Car 1920s
Original specifications (altered by later amendments): wheel base 2740 mm, ground clearance 178 mm; 1170 x 3970 x 1630 mm, weight 712 kgs
Given by James Anderson, 1983
T.1983.23

In 1923, James Anderson of Newton Mearns, near Glasgow, began his quest to create a small, fast sports car that could take part in competitive speed trials as well as road and hill climb competitions. He designed and built a series of experimental motorcars that were light in weight, low in upkeep, and had the road-holding qualities of a much larger vehicle. This Anderson Special Mark II, from the late 1920s, is the only one to have survived. Its design innovations include swing headlamps, a speedometer set directly in the driver's line of sight, a choice of windscreen for different driving conditions and a sealed undercarriage.

CHARLES RENNIE MACKINTOSH AND THE GLASGOW STYLE

'The Glasgow Style' is the collective title given to a distinctive form of decorative art produced by Glasgow designers between 1890 and 1920. It centred around the Glasgow School of Art and the work of architect and designer Charles Rennie Mackintosh. Its most identifiable characteristics are the interplay of sinuous curves and taut lines, organically inspired motifs, such as roses, plants, butterflies, and stylized shapes and forms – hearts, birds and elongated figures.

This gallery displays some of Glasgow Museums' important collection of work by Mackintosh and his Glasgow Style contemporaries. Here you can see objects by craftspeople working across a breadth of decorative media, from jewellery, embroidery and stained glass to furnished interior sections from Miss Cranston's Ingram Street Tearooms.

O Ye, All Ye, That Walk in Willowwood, from the Room de Luxe in The Willow Tearooms, Sauchiehall Street, Glasgow
1903
Margaret Macdonald Mackintosh (1864–1933)
Painted gesso plaster on hessian, set with glass beads, 1645 x 585 mm
Bought with the generous support of the Heritage Lottery Fund, the Art Fund, the Friends of Glasgow Museums, and the many individuals who contributed to the Public Appeal promoted by *The Herald*, 2001
E.2001.6

The title and subject matter for this gesso panel are taken from sonnets written in 1869 by Pre-Raphaelite poet Dante Gabriel Rossetti. They tell of a bereaved man visiting the enchanted Willowwood, where ghosts of women wander forever in mourning for their loved ones. Sitting by a well, he sees his own lost love's faint reflection appear in the water, and then fade away.

The panel focuses on the ghostly apparitions, giving only visual hints of the man's presence. To the left of the face in the top of the green oval you see his hand touching her reflected image in the water – a motion that creates a rose of concentric ripples – and to the right, his tearful eye.

'Honesty' Mirror c.1896
Frances Macdonald (1873–1921)
Beaten tin over a wooden frame, with mirrored glass, 730 x 736 mm
Given by Mrs Alice Talwin Morris, 1946
E.1946.5.a

The plant with the common name honesty (*Lunaria biennis*) is depicted on this repoussé metal frame. It grows up from a circular seed at the centre base of the frame; its stalks, heart-shaped leaves, delicate flower heads and flat round seedpods encircle the central mirror. Two thin androgynous human figures flank the frame, their long flowing hair and robes merging and entwining with the plant. Both figures point to one central honesty seedpod positioned directly above the mirrored glass panel, indicating that this mirror gives an honest reflection of the user. Perhaps Macdonald is humorously suggesting that her mirror never lies.

**The Wassail, from the Ladies'
Luncheon Room, Ingram Street
Tearooms, Glasgow** 1900
Charles Rennie Mackintosh (1868–1928)
1582 x 4620 mm
Gesso, hessian, scrim, twine, glass beads,
thread, mother-of-pearl, tin leaf
Bought by Glasgow City Council as part
of the Ingram Street Tearooms, 1951
E.1981.177.a–c

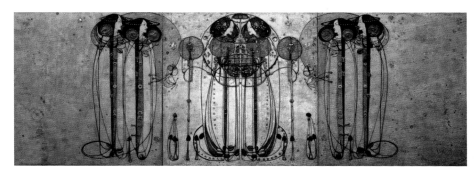

The Wassail is one of two large gesso wall friezes made for tearoom
entrepreneur Miss Catherine Cranston's Ingram Street Tearooms.
The panels were hung high in the room, and so are quite crude in
technique, as if part of a theatrical stage set. Firstly fine gesso plaster
was roughly applied over the loose-weave textile panel. Then outlines
of the figures, plants and trees were added by securing brown painted

string to the canvas with long steel pins.

Wassailing was a pagan fertility ceremony to promote a
successful fruit crop. Amongst his familiar repertoire of forms and motifs
Mackintosh has incorporated symbols with pagan associations, such as
mistletoe and the all-seeing eye, into his design.

**Writing desk for the drawing room, The
Hill House, Helensburgh**
Designed by Charles Rennie Mackintosh, 1904
Made by Alex Martin, 1905
Ebonized mahogany, inset with mother-of-pearl,
ivory and ceramic, decorated with leaded glass
and metal
1125 x 942 (1810 mm open) x 470 mm
Jointly bought with the National Trust for
Scotland, with the generous support of the
Heritage Lottery Fund, the Art Fund, and a
private donor to the National Trust for Scotland,
2002
E.2002.3

(As the desk is co-owned it is only on
display for part of the year.)

This writing desk has a proportional and
musical harmony. Its ebonized surface is
inlaid with luxurious materials that reflect its
composite shapes — squares of mother-of-pearl
on the inside of the square doors and dotted
lines of ivory along the inner curves at the
centre top. These broken lines move the eye
rhythmically and melodiously across the front of
the desk, a movement punctuated by the strong
verticals, or measured beats, of the wooden
compartment dividers. But was music the only
inspiration for Mackintosh's design? The writing
desk's overall shape and proportions are also
very like that of the Japanese kimono.

ART DISCOVERY CENTRE

What is art? What are design, colour, texture? Explore these and other art-related topics in the Art Discovery Centre. This is a space where you can: investigate line, shape and form; use interactive displays to examine objects in depth; put together a mathematical pattern based on Islamic tiles; create a poem about what you think is the mood of a particular painting; or look at patterns in a range of objects.

Lady with a Red Hat 1918
William Strang (1859–1921)
Oil on canvas
1029 x 775 mm
Bought by Glasgow Museums, 1919
1470

The bold colours and the elegant posture of the lady mark this as one of the most striking portraits in the collection. The sitter, Vita Sackville-West, was a famous English aristocrat, poet, gardener and novelist. She was celebrated in society as a member of the Bloomsbury group of intellectuals and even had her lesbian affair with Virginia Woolf immortalized in the latter's novel *Orlando*.

The complementary red and green, reflected in her face, seem brighter when seen side by side, and echo her colourful character. Assertively posed, with elbow extended, she looks every inch the new woman of her time, stylish, confident, an independent thinker.

Two Children 1963
Joan Eardley (1921–63)
Oil and collage on canvas, 1347 x 1347 mm
The unfinished painting was on her easel in the
Townhead studio at the time of her death.
Bought with aid from the National Fund for
Acquisitions and Glasgow Art Gallery and Museums
Association Golden Jubilee Appeal, 1994
3532

One of the principal themes of Eardley's art was the children of the
Townhead area of Glasgow where she had her studio. During the 1960s
she began a series of paintings that depicted them against tenement
walls or shop doorways covered in graffiti and old advertisements. *Two
Children* was Eardley's last and most ambitious picture of the series,
and was found unfinished on her easel after her death at the age of 42
in 1963. Characterized by a restless energy, this bold oil makes good
use of pattern and vivid colour and even incorporates collage (bits of
newspaper and metal foil from sweet wrappers).

LOOKING AT ART

The displays in this gallery are intended as an introduction to the world of visual art. Looking at Art and Art Through a Lens explore the type of subjects that inspire artists and photographers, from favourite people or places to chance events and the vastness of the universe. You can look at the changes that might take place in pictures over the years in Investigating Art, and see how artists sometimes change their minds about their pictures. You will be amazed by an in-focus display on a remarkable amateur artist, John Quinton Pringle, whose painstaking style may be linked to his profession as an optician.

Glasgow Kids, a Saturday Matinee Picture Queue c.1956
Joan Eardley
Oil on canvas, 708 x 1145 mm
Given by the Trustees of the Hamilton Bequest, 1966
3240

In this picture you can see how everyday events in the street lives of poor people in Glasgow fascinated Eardley. She had true sympathy and understanding for them, developed through renting a studio in a slum building just like their homes in Townhead. Eardley was particularly fond of the local children, and painted them in a very down-to-earth manner, which at the time some people felt was unfair or disrespectful. Now her pictures are admired as the best interpretations of slum life, stirring nostalgic memories and even affection for a bygone age.

Regina Cordium (Queen of Hearts) 1866
Dante Gabriel Rossetti (1828–82)
Oil and gold leaf on canvas on panel, 597 x 495 mm
Given by the Trustees of the Hamilton Bequest, 1940
2196

Regina Cordium, translated as Queen of Hearts, is a portrait of Alexa Wilding, whose looks captivated the Pre-Raphaelite painter Rossetti. The picture gives clues about Rossetti's possible feelings for Alexa. The flaming heart and blindfolded Cupid, carrying a bow and arrows, represent love, while the rose and the lily suggest innocence and purity. The composition recalls that of many medieval and Renaissance paintings of the Virgin Mary. Rossetti favoured the styles and techniques of earlier periods, such as the gold background used widely in medieval art. The intense face is a typical vision of Pre-Raphaelite beauty – delicately pale skin and haunting eyes contrast with luscious lips.

VE Day 1945
Laurence Stephen Lowry (1887–1976)
Oil on canvas, 787 x 1016 mm
Bought by Glasgow Museums, 1946
2551

Events he actually witnessed in Manchester, Salford or other towns in the north inspired many of Lowry's pictures. At that time few artists painted ordinary people going about their everyday lives in bleak industrial cities, so his pictures became very popular. In this painting, thousands of 'matchstick' people are seen thronging the streets to celebrate the end of World War II in Europe. The grim industrial buildings are enlivened by flags and bunting, and there are even some people sitting on rooftops. Simply by including so many people, Lowry is able to convey the lively atmosphere of the scene.

The Fairy Raid: Carrying off a changeling — Midsummer Eve 1867
Joseph Noel Paton (1821–1901)

Oil on canvas, 905 x 1467 mm
Given by A. Robertson Cross, 1965
3234

The Victorians were fascinated with fairies and folklore, and many took the subject quite seriously. Although mainly known for his religious subjects, Paton painted some remarkable pictures on this theme. These were immensely popular because of their amazing, meticulous attention to detail. In this lush woodland scene, Paton combines the 'fairy rade', or parade of fairies, with the 'changeling' legend — that fairies could carry off a newborn child, leaving a fairy baby as a substitute. Victorians recognized the contemporary relevance of the subject, as at that time there was much concern over child abduction, human physical deformity, and how this occurred.

**Modern Italy —
The Pifferari** c.1838
Joseph M.W. Turner
(1775–1851)
Oil on canvas
926 x 1232 mm
Given by the sons
of James Reid of
Auchterarder, 1896
733

One of Turner's most romantic and breathtaking landscapes, this vast panorama is bathed in warm, shimmering light and brilliantly luminous colours. Nature overpowers everything. Turner was particularly inspired by Italy and its Roman Catholic traditions. Look for a woman confessing to a monk, and a procession with banners and crucifix, wending its way towards a church. However, the most intriguing element of all is the group (lower left) of *pifferari*, strolling musicians who played every Christmas at wayside shrines and street-corner images of the Madonna in the belief that their music relieved her labour pains.

**Self Portrait in
Stetson** 1989
John Byrne
(b.1940)
Oil on canvas
902 x 705 mm
Bought by
Glasgow
Museums, 1990
3469

A cold Scottish sea in the background of a painting of a cowboy is a clue that this is not Kentucky! A pair of red braces and a stetson hat were given to Paisley-born painter and writer John Byrne in 1979. He felt that it 'seemed natural to put them together and do a self portrait as a cowpoke' — a wry comment on how many Glaswegians imagine themselves as cowboys. The work was painted while he was writing his play *Your Cheatin' Heart*. If you stare long enough, you can almost hear Willie Nelson singing, with seagulls.

Windows in the West® 1993
Avril Paton® (b.1941)
Watercolour, 1220 x 1520 mm
Bought by Glasgow Museums, 1994
PR.1994.16

One of the most popular Kelvingrove pictures, probably because of its local connections, *Windows in the West* was inspired by a chance event that captured the artist's imagination. One January evening there was a freak snowstorm, which lasted 10 minutes. The view from Paton's studio window in Glasgow's Athole Gardens, looking onto Saltoun Street, was transformed. Where there had been darkness, suddenly there was bright whiteness. Paton brilliantly details the glowing interiors of the tenement building with people going about their everyday lives. This warmth is contrasted with the coldness of the wintry scene outside and the lilac-pink sky.

Two Figures at a Fence 1904, John Q. Pringle (1864–1925)
Oil on canvas, 254 x 305 mm, Given by John W. Pringle, 1947
2662

John Quinton Pringle is one of Glasgow's greatest artistic secrets. He was an optician by trade, and a repairer of scientific instruments, who took up art in his spare time. In Kelvingrove you can see the largest selection anywhere of his paintings and miniatures, from his early, slightly naïve efforts to the highly accomplished works done at the end of his life. You can chart his improvement, as he gained skill and confidence by attending classes at the Glasgow School of Art.

Pringle's unique style, with its emphasis on intense surface detail, owed a lot to his daytime job, working under the microscope. The most intriguing element of his painting, with its characteristic spotty surface, is its unexplained similarity to the work of French Post-Impressionists such as Signac. Pringle spent only ten days in France, in 1910; but he was an avid exhibition-goer in Glasgow and London, aware of the latest artistic developments. Pringle's paintings give a fascinating view of his life through the people and places he knew in Glasgow's East End and from his holiday visits to Islay, Normandy and Shetland.

THE EXPRESSION COURT

The displays in the Expression Court are essentially about the power and diversity of human communication and artistic expression. Here we explore some of the disparate ways in which we send and receive messages, and how our different senses process these messages to make meaning and to move us emotionally. The music of the orchestrion, the dance masquerade interactive, and the soundtrack of human speech add the element of sound to the otherwise visual displays. While the majority of the seven displays do feature human communication, the inclusion of Animal Speak recognizes that communication, for one reason or another, is important for all life. The gallery's theme of 'expression' is reflected by the suspended *Heads* installation, which links to the marble busts on open display on the gallery floor below.

Prince Min, guardian roof tile

Ming dynasty
(1368–1644)
Earthenware
decorated with over-
glaze enamels
450 x 254 x 140 mm
Given by Sir William
and Lady Burrell,
1946
38.522

The angry, muscular figure on this ridge tile may be Prince Min of the Chinese state of Qi. In 283 BC, his disastrous 18-year reign ended with a terrible death — he was hung from the roof for three days on the Prime Minister's orders, his skin peeled off by soldiers and his tendons ripped out. His successors placed a pottery effigy on the roof ridge as protection against his evil spirit returning.

In Chinese traditions, a roof marked the point of intersection between heaven and earth. Roof ridges were curved from the Han dynasty (206 BC–AD 220) onwards, as it was believed that spirits could only move in straight lines. Roof tiles were placed on temples and private buildings to ward off evil spirits and bring good luck. The figure of Min Wang is still seen on many buildings in China. Sir William Burrell bought this figure in 1946 for £41, from London dealer John Sparks.

Wives of Fishermen

c.1914
Pierre Braecke
(1858–1938)
Marble
1155 x 755 x 440 mm
Bought by Glasgow
Museums, 1923
S.151

The tragic story behind this sculpture is plain to see. Four women wait anxiously for the return of their husbands from a storm at sea, hope fading. Their plain clothing and wooden clogs indicate the poverty as well as the tough lives of Belgian fisher folk.

Braecke chose a block of grey marble, whose diagonal pattern and sombre colour suggest the harsh effects of the icy wind and rain. Artists do not always choose physical beauty when searching for a subject. As this sculpture shows so powerfully, a painful or difficult aspect of life can result in a work of art that touches us all.

The Heads 2006

Designed by Sophy Cave, Event Communications
Manufactured in fibreglass by MDM of London

The Heads were designed to imitate the freedom of visitors' thoughts and ideas, drifting from the centre of the Expression Court out into the perimeter galleries — imagine letting off a load of balloons and watching them float off at random.

The faces reflect multiple human expressions. Only four were cast, but when viewed en masse, and from different angles, they appear like so many more.

The installation was designed to be enjoyed from all aspects, and to prompt individual responses from visitors as they make their way through the galleries, viewing both *The Heads* and the Kelvingrove collections from many different perspectives.

'Cottage' Orchestrion, No. 3 1887

Michael Welte & Söhne
A.1942.34.1

This rare, finely made Michael Welte & Söhne 'Cottage' Orchestrion, No. 3, was built at the firm's Freiburg factory in Germany during the late nineteenth century. Described as a masterpiece of engineering, the instrument has a weight-driven pulley, operated by a windlass, that activates the main bellows. Perforated music rolls emulate the sounds of an orchestra — hence the name — through numerous, delicately voiced pipes. As well as the melody, the orchestrion produces the sounds of kettle, snare and bass drums, triangle and cymbal. A collection of rolls, the invention of the maker, includes works by Bizet, Strauss, Handel and Wagner.

GLASGOW STORIES

We intend to change the displays regularly in this gallery to give some insights into the complex and multi-layered city that is Glasgow. This gallery has given us an opportunity to respond to public requests for thought-provoking displays and those that make links between Glasgow and the rest of the world.

From James Watt's inventive genius to the desperate plight of some of our citizens, as shown in Violence Against Women and Glasgow in Mind, we have chosen a broad sweep of experiences. Symbols that Divide tells a story unique to this city, as does I belong to Glasgow. Meanwhile, Glasgow and the Wild West presents a glimpse of our less serious side. All these stories are rooted in history, but told from a contemporary perspective.

Brank 16th century
Iron, 60 x 180 x 410 mm
1902.73.ni

Branks are derived from horse bridles. These were not all designed in the same way, but the end result was to control, silence or punish the wearer. In Scotland they were used on women accused of witchcraft during the sixteenth century, a time when fear of sorcery was at its height. The victim would be paraded through the town wearing the brank to prevent her from cursing the spectators. Once there, the chain was used to fix the victim to a stake or perhaps to the market cross. They were also used as a punishment for women accused of adultery. The spike was designed to fit over and depress a woman's tongue. These devices continued to be used as gags for nagging wives into the nineteenth century.

Buffalo Bill objects
Given by George C. Crager, 1892

Necklace 1880s
Otter skin and grizzly bear claws with pendant of ermine and brass bells
810 x 380 x 50 mm
1892.2.h

Shield
1880s
Buckskin
380 mm
1892.3.n

Moccasins 1880s
Buckskin and beadwork
110 x 230 x 90 mm
1892.3.b.[1] & [2]

Buffalo Bill's Wild West Show first came to Glasgow in 1891. It was based in the East End Exhibition Building, a remnant from the previous year's Industrial Exhibition and remodelled for this purpose. For three months Glaswegians were treated to the sight of the stars of the show walking the streets of their city – imagine what a stir that must have caused.

Some of these stars were Native Americans who chose to join the show rather than spend time in prison after being captured at the Battle of Wounded Knee in 1890. Short Bull, the owner of this necklace and one of the leaders of the Ghost Dance, was one of those. Another star, Lone Bull, made this shield, while the moccasins are said to have been taken from a dead warrior, Across-the-Room, son of Big Foot, chief of a band of Hunkpapa Lakota massacred at Wounded Knee. (See also the modern Ghost Dance shirt, p.67.)

The show's interpreter, George C. Crager, gave the city's museum a selection of artefacts before the show left. These now form the core of our Native American collection.

Figure of St Patrick
2080 x 890 x
740 mm
PP.1985.218

Orange Lodge banner
mid-20th century
Silk, 2430 x 2180 mm
PP.1984.172

This statue of St Patrick, patron saint of Ireland, was taken from the church of St Joseph, North Woodside Road, Glasgow, before it was demolished. St Patrick wears a mitre on his head and carries a crozier – the symbols of a bishop or abbot. His right hand is raised in a gesture of blessing and his downward gaze is directed towards the faithful. A snake is coiled around the bottom of his crozier – legend tells that St Patrick drove the snakes out of Ireland. He is a popular symbol of the Irish, Catholic and Protestant alike, and is celebrated around the world on St Patrick's Day, 17 March.

The banner was used in marches by the Loyal Orange Lodge of Rutherglen, (L.O.L. number 246). The Orange Order was set up in Ireland in 1795 to defend the Protestant faith, and members celebrate the Battle of the Boyne each year on 12 July. The banner shows King William III on a white horse ordering his army across the River Boyne in Ireland in a battle where he defeated the Catholic King James VII and II in 1690. The king is wearing an orange sash, symbolic of the House of Orange, the Dutch royal family.

Model of a James Watt beam engine
late 1800s
1100 x 870 x 470 mm
1908.40

This model was probably made in the late nineteenth century to help teachers demonstrate James Watt's steam engine. Watt himself worked with models of steam engines. Indeed, legend tells of a time when he was young and had been asked by Glasgow University professors to repair a model steam engine. Watt went for a walk on Glasgow Green to consider the work ahead, and while on this walk found his inspiration to alter the model to improve its performance. The changes he made created a new type of steam engine that was to change the world.

ANCIENT EGYPT

The Ancient Egypt gallery tells the story of life, death and rebirth in Ancient Egypt in three linked displays. It includes many treasures from the British Museum's study collection, displayed through their Partnership UK scheme and the generosity of the Dorset Foundation. Jobs for the Boys and Jobs for the Girls in Ancient Egypt contrast the very different prospects in life for men and women at that time. At the centre of the gallery, the sarcophagus of Pabasa and the coffin and mummy of Ankhesnefer provide a focus for How to Survive Death the Ancient Egyptian Way, a guide to living forever in the afterlife. Gods of the Living and the Dead explores the myth of Osiris, the Egyptians' explanation for the mysteries of life and death, order and chaos, this world and the next.

Sarcophagus of Pabasa Late Period, 26th dynasty, reign of Psamtek I, probably 656–640 BC
Granite stone
1200 x 2400 x 750 mm
Given by the Hamilton Estates Trustees, 1922
1922.86

The massive sarcophagus of Pabasa was found in tomb TT279, in the Asasif, Western Thebes, by Giovanni d'Athanasi. Pabasa was the most powerful male official of his day in Upper Egypt. King Psamtek I appointed him as Great Steward to his virgin daughter, Nitocris, who, as God's Wife of Amun, ruled Upper Egypt on the pharaoh's behalf. D'Athanasi sold the sarcophagus to Alexander, 10th Duke of Hamilton, and in 1834 it was installed in the Egyptian Hall of Hamilton Palace, near Glasgow. It remained there until 1919 when the building, undermined by coal workings, was demolished. The sarcophagus was given to Glasgow Museums by the Trustees of the Hamilton Estates in 1922, and has been on public display in Kelvingrove ever since. Duke Alexander himself was mummified and buried in another Egyptian sarcophagus in Hamilton Mausoleum.

ENVIRONMENT DISCOVERY CENTRE

Here you can explore the fascinating world around us. You can get hands-on and use a magnifying glass to look closely at insects, fossils and rocks; examine different kinds of seeds, and how they are scattered far and wide; watch the bees in their hive; explore how animals move and feed; find out all about red squirrels; fit a model brain in a fox and find out why we have a spine; look at the amazing variety of shell shapes and sizes, colours and patterns, and the creatures that live in shells; discover biodiversity and evolution in Scotland and beyond.

The observation beehive

Kelvingrove's honeybees, *Apis mellifera*, have a special place in our visitors' hearts. We have kept bees since 1959, and work closely with local beekeepers to offer them the best possible care. During our refurbishment, they moved to hives in the north-east of Glasgow. Reinstated soon after we reopened in 2006, they now live in an observation hive custom-built by our joiners. Being living creatures, they sometimes surprise — in the 1980s they swarmed and came to rest above a group of sunbathers on the adjacent bowling green. Without his beekeeping equipment to hand, the beekeeper needed a creative solution — sunbathers watched in bewilderment as he collected the swarm in his motorbike helmet and gloves!

Thanks to Charles Irwin, Glasgow and District Beekeepers Association

Honeybees, *Apis mellifera*, in the observation beehive

SCOTLAND'S WILDLIFE

Scotland's varied and beautiful landscape is home to some of Britain's rarest and most inspiring wildlife. Some varieties of animals and plants are found nowhere else in the world. And wherever we live, we can find interesting things, even in a big bustling city like Glasgow. In this gallery you can find out about the wildlife that lives in Scotland, from the bottom of our lochs and high up in our mountains, to quite literally on our doorsteps. There are species that may be very familiar, but we hope you will enjoy finding out about those you may not know so well.

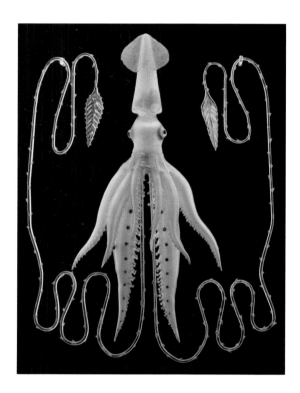

Glass model of long-armed squid *Chiroteuthis veranyi* 1880s
Dresden, Germany
220 x 185 x 60 mm
Bought from Mrs P.B. Mason, 1909
1909.66.js

Glasgow Museums has a small but rare collection of marine animals made from glass. In the late 1800s Leopold and Rudolph Blaschka made a wide range of botanical and zoological models. They studied live animals in aquariums before making amazingly life-like replicas. Museums and universities used these models as teaching aids, but now they are also appreciated as works of art.

There are several Blaschka models in this gallery, including sea slugs, jellyfish and sea anemones, although this beautiful, delicate model of a long-armed squid is displayed in the Study Centre. This squid is found in seas and oceans around the world, and has some of the longest tentacles in proportion to its size of any cephalopod. The collection was bought from Mrs P.B. Mason for £275 in 1909.

Dried pike head *Esox lucius* 1934
Endrick Marshes, Loch Lomond, Scotland
155 x 365 x 185 mm
Given by Major G.H. Christie
Z.1969.93.1

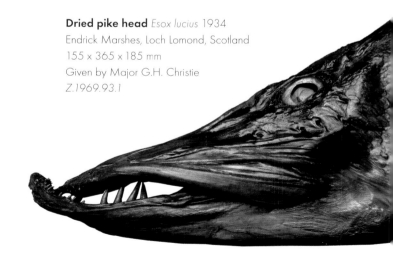

This head is all that remains of a large female pike found dead where the River Endrick flows into Loch Lomond. It had been left stranded after the area flooded in about 1934. The head has become the source of legend amongst fishermen from all over the world. Nobody knows how big the original fish was, but some have estimated that it could have weighed over 31kg (around 70 lbs). As the current Scottish record is only 21.6 kg (47lb 11oz) this is possibly wishful thinking!

Pike are large predatory fish found throughout the northern hemisphere. They are very popular with fishermen due to their aggressive nature.

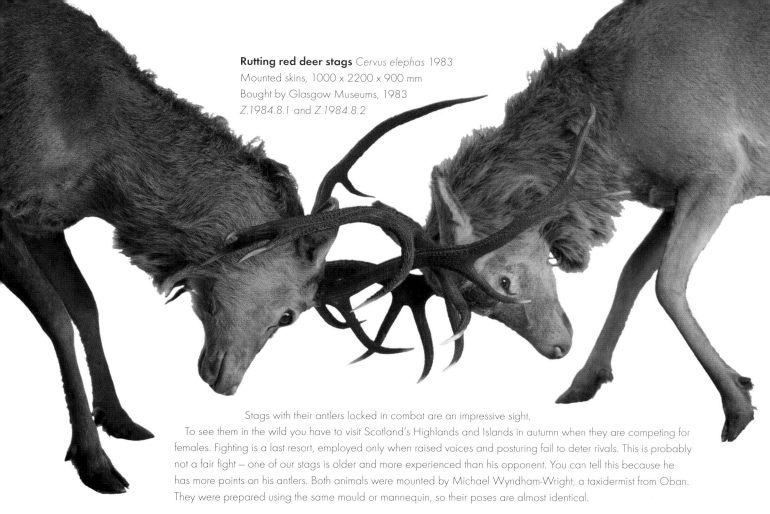

Rutting red deer stags *Cervus elephas* 1983
Mounted skins, 1000 x 2200 x 900 mm
Bought by Glasgow Museums, 1983
Z.1984.8.1 and Z.1984.8.2

Stags with their antlers locked in combat are an impressive sight.
To see them in the wild you have to visit Scotland's Highlands and Islands in autumn when they are competing for females. Fighting is a last resort, employed only when raised voices and posturing fail to deter rivals. This is probably not a fair fight — one of our stags is older and more experienced than his opponent. You can tell this because he has more points on his antlers. Both animals were mounted by Michael Wyndham-Wright, a taxidermist from Oban. They were prepared using the same mould or mannequin, so their poses are almost identical.

Ruddy Duck
Oxyura jamaicensis
2005
Coatbridge, Scotland
Adult male, mounted skin
220 x 220 x 160 mm
Given by R. Sutcliffe, 2005
DB.8286

The ruddy duck is a North American species that escaped from captivity in England between 1956 and 1963 and started to breed in Britain. There are now about 4,000 of them here and it has also spread to mainland Europe. In Spain it started to breed with the closely related and endangered white-headed duck, producing a hybrid which threatened to wipe it out. A controversial decision was made to cull ruddy ducks in Britain. We tried to obtain one of the culled birds for the museum without success, but luckily for us (although not for the bird!) this one was hit by a car near Coatbridge, Lanarkshire.

THE LIFE COURT

Although dominated by Glasgow's Spitfire LA198, much of this gallery is devoted to natural history. The diversity of animals and plants is explored in Nature's Record Breakers, while Sir Roger, the Asian elephant, is one of Kelvingrove's iconic objects — as is the skeleton of the Baron of Buchlyvie, a famous Clydesdale horse.

Fulton's orrery, dating from 1833, demonstrates the movements of the solar system. There are stories about charms and healing and beautiful minerals, and a painting of the Clyde by John Knox is used to explain the local geology. Insects fly upwards to join a flock of flying birds and a model of Percy Pilcher's glider, 'Gull', near the ceiling.

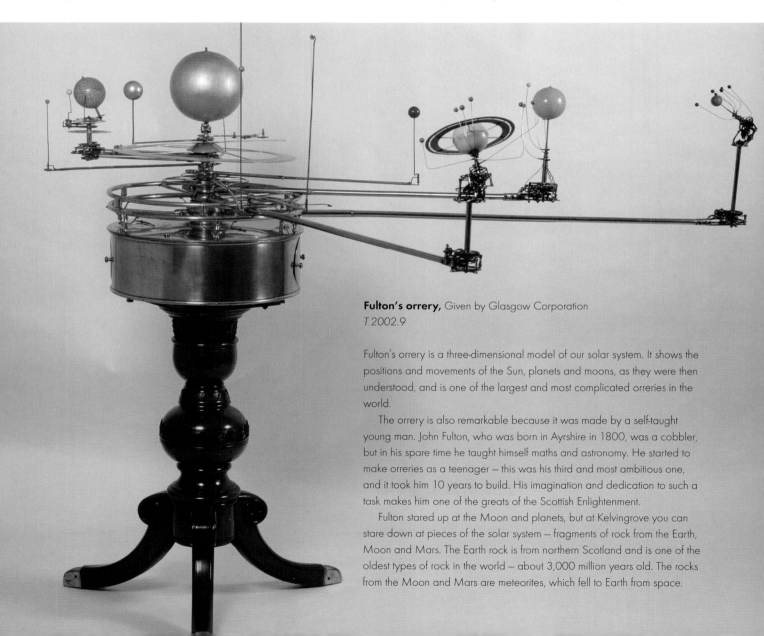

Fulton's orrery, Given by Glasgow Corporation
T.2002.9

Fulton's orrery is a three-dimensional model of our solar system. It shows the positions and movements of the Sun, planets and moons, as they were then understood, and is one of the largest and most complicated orreries in the world.

The orrery is also remarkable because it was made by a self-taught young man. John Fulton, who was born in Ayrshire in 1800, was a cobbler, but in his spare time he taught himself maths and astronomy. He started to make orreries as a teenager — this was his third and most ambitious one, and it took him 10 years to build. His imagination and dedication to such a task makes him one of the greats of the Scottish Enlightenment.

Fulton stared up at the Moon and planets, but at Kelvingrove you can stare down at pieces of the solar system — fragments of rock from the Earth, Moon and Mars. The Earth rock is from northern Scotland and is one of the oldest types of rock in the world — about 3,000 million years old. The rocks from the Moon and Mars are meteorites, which fell to Earth from space.

Vickers-Armstrong Supermarine Spitfire LA198 1944
Length: 32 feet 8 inches;
wingspan 36 feet 11 inches
T.1999.14

As a Mark 21 Spitfire, this aeroplane's Griffon 61 engine allowed it to achieve a top speed of 442 miles per hour during its first test flight. Spitfire LA198 survived the war because it crashed on landing on its return to Horsham St Faith Base on 22 July 1949. It might have been sold, like so many others, had it been undamaged.

   The aeroplane was returned to the City of Glasgow in 1998, parliamentary approval having been given in 1996, and the Scottish Executive supplied a budget to restore and display it. We are very proud to be able to exhibit this magnificent aeroplane as a symbol of Glasgow's achievements, an acknowledgement of the heroism of her people, and a reminder of her history.

   The restoration of the Spitfire was a joint project between Glasgow Museums and National Museums Scotland funded by the Scottish Executive

Scottish Minerals

Scotland has a rich mineral heritage. To the left are just two examples. Galena, the major ore of lead, here forms a fine specimen along with quartz. Leadhills and Wanlockhead, high in the Lowther Hills, were once at the centre of Scotland's most important lead mining industry. Copper, silver and zinc were also mined in the hills around these villages, and gold has been found in stream deposits. For the mineral collector, the main interest of the area is in the wide range of different minerals, including rare types, found here. These include leadhillite, lanarkite and caledonite, all named after their first discovery at this locality.

   Prehnite is a speciality of the Glasgow area, and this example is typical of the excellent, pale green specimens that have been found at several places near the city. Around 340 million years ago there were active volcanoes here, and the lava flows that erupted at this time today form the Kilpatrick, Campsie and other hills near the city. Prehnite, along with several other minerals such as calcite, heulandite and stilbite, formed in cracks and cavities in the lava after it had solidified.

Galena and quartz
Leadhills, South
Lanarkshire
250 x 190 mm
Given by Dr N. Holgate,
1959
G.1959.47.d

Prehnite
Bowling Quarry
West Dunbartonshire
115 x 50 mm
Given by R. Barstow,
1979
G.1979.176.6

THE LIFE COURT

Sir Roger, mounted Asian Elephant
Elephas maximus 1900
2800 x 3300 x 1200 mm
Given by E.H. Bostock
1900.170

The star of Kelvingrove's natural history
collections, Sir Roger has been one of the
most popular and permanent fixtures since
the museum opened in 1901. He toured
the country with Bostock & Wombwell's
Menagerie in the 1890s, then moved to the
Scottish Zoo in Glasgow. Unfortunately he
became dangerous and had to be put down.

    Sir Roger was mounted by the taxidermy
firm of Charles Kirk & Co., who had to remove
their whole shop front in order to get him out
when they were finished. Over the years he
has appeared on TV, featured in magazines
and newspapers and been the source of
many a local urban myth.

Dried Japanese Spider Crab *Macrocheira kaempferi* 1907
Japanese seas, 950 x 1600 x 250 mm
Given by Mrs Murdoch
1907.48

This crab is the biggest invertebrate in Glasgow's collections,
and also the biggest type of crab in the world. Although scary
to look at, it is really a gentle giant that feeds on dead animals
and shellfish on the seabed. In life they hold their bodies up
rather than lying flat like this one.

    It only lives in the deep seas around Japan, where it is
fished and eaten as a delicacy. These crabs were greatly
admired by museums and collectors in Victorian times. Today
they are found in aquariums around the world as their 'alien'
appearance makes them very popular with visitors.

Cheetah *Acinonyx jubatus* 2004
Mounted skin
970 x 1450 x 460 mm
Given by National Museums Scotland, 2006
Z.2008.6

The cheetah is the fastest land mammal in the world, regularly running at speeds of up to 65 miles (105 km) per hour in short bursts, when chasing its prey. It may sometimes reach 75 miles (120km) per hour.

We had great difficulty in obtaining a cheetah for Kelvingrove. Most cheetahs that die in British zoos are post-mortemed by zoo vets, and are therefore not in good enough condition to be mounted for display. Eventually we managed to get this one from Whipsnade Zoo, where it had died of natural causes due to kidney failure.

Baron of Buchlyvie, skeleton of Clydesdale horse *Equus cabalus*
1914
1950 x 2600 x 1500 mm
Given by William Dunlop
1918.54

The Baron of Buchlyvie was one of the most famous Clydesdale horses of his time. Due to a legal dispute over his ownership, he became the talk of the nation. This dispute was resolved by an auction in 1911, at which he fetched £9,500 – a record amount for the time.

The Baron was put down in 1914 after a mare broke his leg. He was buried in his owner's rose garden, but eventually dug up and donated to Glasgow Museums. He has been immortalized in paintings and songs, and his offspring went on to become champions.

DUTCH ART

The Dutch Art gallery features paintings made in the Netherlands between about 1600 and 1730 – the 'Golden Age' of Dutch painting. There are eight themes. Seafaring, Trade and Prosperity highlights the crucial importance of the sea to Dutch wealth and culture. Not to be missed is Rembrandt's Man in Armour, which explores one of Glasgow's greatest treasures. The Dutch and Religion features religious subjects and church interiors. Everyday Life? looks at portraiture and domestic scenes – often with a moral message. Landscapes and the Art Market considers how economic factors shaped art. Still Lifes includes 'breakfast pieces' and flower paintings. The final two sections are Flemish Painting, with masterpieces by Rubens and Jordaens, and Gerard de Lairesse's *Allegory of the Senses*.

A Country Gathering by a Bridge c.1660–65
Nicolaes Berchem
(1621/22–83)
Oil on canvas
733 x 987 mm
Bequeathed by
Mrs John Graham-
Gilbert, 1877
566

Berchem's *Country Gathering* is among the finest Dutch landscapes in Glasgow. The artist was one of the leading painters of Dutch 'Italianate' landscapes – scenes bathed in the warm light of Italy, and usually featuring motifs and figures drawn from the Italian countryside. Such subjects were first painted in about 1620 by Dutch artists working in Rome, and continued to be produced by them and their followers, both in Italy and back home, until the end of seventeenth century.

The appeal of this picture lies in the charm of its anecdotal details, the decorative flourish of the composition and, above all, the brilliant evocation of the intense heat and light of the Mediterranean sun.

A Man in Armour
1655 or 1659
Harmensz van Rijn
Rembrandt
(1606–69)
Oil on canvas
1375 x 1045 mm
Bequeathed by
Mrs John Graham-
Gilbert, 1877
601

A Man in Armour – a masterpiece by Rembrandt, the greatest Dutch artist of his age – is the most famous and best-loved seventeenth-century Dutch painting in Glasgow.

Out of a dark and impenetrable background, Rembrandt conjures up an image of a young man, weighed down both by with his thoughts and his gleaming breastplate, elaborate helmet and lance. But who is this man? One important clue is the owl motif on the antique-looking helmet, which is probably to be identified as a symbol of Athene (Minerva). As goddess of war, she was revered by all soldiers in classical antiquity, including Alexander the Great, the most successful general of them all.

An Allegory of the Senses
1668
Gerard de Lairesse
(1641–1711)
Oil on canvas
1372 x 1829 mm
Bought with assistance from the Heritage Lottery Fund, Art Fund, and the Trustees of the Hamilton Bequest, 2001
3635

The Senses are represented in this painting by the five main figures, each of whom holds or does something associated with a particular sense – sight, touch, hearing, taste and smell. But, just as the senses are short-lived – like the magnificent array of fruit and flowers nearby – so true love, symbolized by the statue of Cupid on the right, is eternal.

Such a grand and moralizing painting was probably commissioned by someone both wealthy and learned. It may have been a member of the Van Rijn family, whose children are said to have been the models for those in this picture. In 1730, an Elizabeth van Rijn married Jacques-Philippe d'Orville, a celebrated Amsterdam professor, from whose descendants this painting was bought in 2001. It is by far the most important addition to the Dutch Art collection in over a hundred years.

Flowers in a Terracotta Vase 1723
Rachel Ruysch (1664–1750), Oil on canvas, 394 x 314 mm, Bequeathed by Archibald McLellan, 1854
82

Ruysch painted this work in 1723, when she was nearly 60 – still more than 20 years from the end of an extraordinarily long career as a specialist painter of flower and fruit still lifes. These subjects were regarded as particularly suitable for female artists, who were banned from studying the figure in life drawing classes. Ruysch was one of very few professional female artists of her day, but an exceptionally successful one.

She had the advantage of coming from a wealthy and highly educated family – her father was an internationally famous botanist and anatomist. Her inherited curiosity about the natural world is evident in every meticulously painted detail of this piece. Recent conservation work revealed once more the sheer beauty of the various flowers, and the convincing illusion of their forms in space.

ITALIAN ART

This gallery features arts of the Renaissance period, from about 1400 to 1600. Most of the exhibits were produced in Italy, but there are also a few paintings from Northern Europe that show an Italian influence. As well as paintings, the gallery includes high-class arms and armour, brilliantly decorated ceramics and luxurious glassware.

The objects are displayed by themes — Made in Venice, Beautiful Things, which looks at the ownership of art as a status symbol, and The Art of War, which underlines the constant backdrop of warfare that characterized this artistic period. The Craft of Art illustrates methods and raw materials used by artists, and the New Perspectives audiovisual display demonstrates advances made in the depiction of three-dimensional space.

The Adulteress brought before Christ and **Head of a Man** c.1509
Tiziano Vecellio, known as Titian (c.1487/90–1576)
Oil on canvas, 1390 x 182 mm and 470 x 410 mm
Main painting bequeathed by Archibald McLellan, 1854; *Head of a Man* bought by Glasgow Museums, 1971
181 and 3283

These two paintings were once part of the same work. Notice the disembodied knee in striped hose on the extreme right-hand side of the main picture — this leg once belonged to the man whose head has been detached to make a separate work. We do not know when or why this was done, but perhaps this corner of the work was damaged.

The main painting was bequeathed by Archibald McLellan in 1854, together with many other wonderful works of art. The separated head was bought much later, in 1971. For many years the work was thought to have been painted by Giorgione, but we now think it is by Titian, one of his pupils.

The Annunciation c.1493
Sandro Botticelli (c.1445–1510)
Tempera and gold on a wooden panel
510 x 620 mm
Bequeathed by Archibald McLellan, 1854
174

In this wonderfully realistic depiction of three-dimensional space, the Angel Gabriel hurries to tell the Virgin Mary that she is to bear God's son, Jesus. As rays of gold representing God's grace radiate towards her, Mary's modest pose and humble bow indicate that she has accepted this precious mission.

A barely legible inscription on the reverse of this painting tells us that it was originally hung in the church of St Barnabas in Florence. However, we know that this work was brought out of Italy in 1832, some time before interest in early Renaissance painting had become really fashionable in Britain.

Madonna and Child
c.1483
Giovanni Bellini
(c.1430–1516)
Oil paint on wooden panel
610 x 470 mm
Bequeathed by Mrs John Graham Gilbert, 1877
575

This picture shares a tender, intimate moment between mother and son with the viewer. It would originally have been placed high up inside a church, and worshippers would have seen Mary and Jesus gazing down at them, with Jesus making a gesture representing Christian blessing. Mary's sad expression shows us that she is thinking about the future suffering of her son.

The painting was bequeathed to the City of Glasgow's collection in 1877 by the widow of John Graham-Gilbert, a Glaswegian artist who had lived in Italy for several years as a young man. We once thought that the dark colour behind the figures hid a more detailed background, but X-rays have shown that this was not the case.

The Avant armour — Milanese field armour c.1440
Italian, steel, leather, 1680 x 745 x 485 mm, Given by R.L. Scott, 1939
E.1939.65.e

Made around 1440, this is one of the oldest near-complete armours in the world and is in remarkably good condition. It remained in the castle armoury of a noble family in the Alps until an American media tycoon bought it in the early twentieth century. It is often called the 'Avant' armour, because this word, meaning 'Forward!', is inscribed on the edges of the breastplate. The armour was made in the renowned armour-making city of Milan, in Italy. Armours made by Milanese craftsmen were greatly sought after by wealthy warriors all across Europe. This beautifully shaped war armour was made to fit its owner perfectly so as not to impede manoeuvrability, and provided excellent protection against the various weapons used on the medieval battlefield. Certain parts of the armour are almost four millimetres thick.

Technology, design, and decoration combine to create protection that is both aesthetically pleasing — with its rounded forms — and functional, with features such as applied stop ribs to deflect the attack of incoming blades. With religious inscriptions inscribed on the armour, and the quality of the steel skilfully tempered by its Milanese craftsmen, the wearer would confidently go forward into battle.

St Lawrence c.1373
Niccolò di Buonaccorso (c.1348–88)
Tempera and gold on a wooden panel
630 x 310 mm
Given by Julius Lewis Lyons, 1980
3359

We can tell from the size and shape of this panel that it once formed part of a large altarpiece of the type found in and around Siena in the late fourteenth century. The panel is enriched with real gold and shows St Lawrence, a Christian deacon in third-century Rome. He is holding his attributes — the objects that identify him. The palm frond tells us that he was a martyr, killed for his faith, and in his right hand is a gridiron, on which he is said to have been roasted alive.

The painting was given to the collection by Julius Lewis Lyons, who lent, donated and bequeathed many other valuable objects to Glasgow over the years, including silver, antiquities and old master drawings.

Bowl, wineglass and plate 16th century, Venice, Italy, Glass
Bowl 125 x 175 mm; wineglass 163 x 102 mm; plate 265 x 265 mm
Bought separately: bowl in 1893; wineglass in 1896; the plate with the assistance of grants from the Local Museums Purchase Fund and the Art Fund, 1980
1893.93.y, 1896.38.b, E.1980.64

Venice is famous for decorative glass. The finest pieces have always been treasured by collectors and Glasgow Museums has some beautiful examples.

These three fragile vessels show some of the different shapes and techniques used in the manufacture of high-quality Venetian glass during the Renaissance period.

The brightly-coloured bowl was made to imitate a naturally-occurring stone called chalcedony. It would have been inspired by rare surviving examples from the Ancient Roman period, and was mounted in gilt metal later. The stemmed wineglass is quite clear. The name of this type of glass in Italian is *cristallo*, meaning 'crystal'. It is feather light, and has miraculously survived for well over 400 years. The white glass plate is also very rare and precious – only five others are known. Its delicate decoration was carefully engraved using a diamond point, and the individual sections outlined in gold.

The bowl and wine glass were purchased for the collection in the late nineteenth century, when the vogue for collecting Italian Renaissance-period items for museums was at its height. The transparent plate once belonged to the Earl of Clanwilliam, and was bought relatively recently, in 1980.

Plate showing the story of Apollo and Daphne,
c.1530
Painted by Francesco Xanto Avelli (c.1487–1542)
Tin-glazed earthenware, maiolica
20 x 260 x 260 mm
Bought by Glasgow Museums, 1893
1893.93.a

Plates like this one would have been more for display than everyday use at table. An inscription on the back tells us that the Greek god Apollo is chasing Daphne, the girl he loves. To avoid Apollo's unwanted attentions Daphne is dramatically changed into a laurel tree by her father, a river god, who looks on.

The most important European ceramic item in Glasgow, this plate once belonged to Frédéric Spitzer's fabulous collection of medieval art. Although this was a private collection, Spitzer opened it to public view in Paris. The plate was bought for Glasgow's collections, along with other items, at Spitzer's famous auction sale held in 1893.

FRENCH ART

Glasgow has an internationally important collection of French art. In this gallery you can see how French painting changed in the nineteenth and early twentieth centuries. Among the themes explored are the challenges that artists face when they choose to work out of doors, paint someone's portrait or pick a particular viewpoint.

We have hung some paintings at a lower height so that our younger visitors are able to get close to them. One painting not to miss is Van Gogh's portrait of Scottish art dealer Alex Reid. Reid brought many of these paintings to Scotland and persuaded collectors such as William McInnes to buy them.

The Young Girls c.1885
Mary Cassatt (1844–1926)
Oil on canvas, 465 x 560 mm
Given by the Trustees of the Hamilton Bequest, 1953
2980

Mary Cassatt is famous for her sensitive paintings of mothers and children. Although she herself never married or had children of her own, she was constantly surrounded by the many children of her family and friends. Who are these two children? Are they sisters? Frustratingly, we do not know. Is Cassatt saying something about the innocence of childhood, rather than painting a particular portrait? Although the painting is signed it has a sketchy, rather unfinished look. This may be deliberate. The freshness and vitality of the brushwork and the naturalness of the girls' pose gives this painting an essentially modern character, a feeling of the immediacy of everyday life.

Portrait of Alexander Reid 1887
Vincent van Gogh (1853–90)
Oil on board, 410 x 329 mm
Bought with the aid of a special Government grant, the Art Fund, an anonymous donor and public subscription, 1974
3315

Animated by fiery touches of red, orange and green, this portrait has an enigmatic and expressive power. Reid worked in Paris with Van Gogh's art dealer brother Theo and, for a short while, shared the brothers' Montmartre apartment. Until 1928 this was believed to be a self-portrait of Van Gogh. Reid's son saw the painting in a catalogue, contacted the artist's family and told them it was actually a portrait of his father. Why the confusion? An artist friend of Reid and Vincent wrote that the two men were so alike that 'they might have been twins. I have often hesitated, until I got close, as to which of them I was meeting'.

Vétheuil 1880
Claude Monet (1840–1926)
Oil on canvas, 600 x 806 mm
Bequeathed by William McInnes, 1944
2403

This is a truly Impressionist painting. Monet painted it outside, directly on to the canvas, and in just a few hours. Using small, hasty brushstrokes, he strives to capture the fleeting effects of light and movement on the ever-changing scene in front of him. His brushstrokes do not differentiate between the varying textures of sky, water and trees – they are all painted alike. Sometimes it is even difficult just to know what we are seeing – for instance, the lively strokes of red that dance in the foreground are poppies! Despite the carefree look of this summer landscape, this work was painted just after the death of Monet's wife Camille.

Poor Fauvette 1881, Jules Bastien-Lepage (1848–84)
Oil on canvas, 1625 x 1257 mm
Bought by Glasgow Museums, 1913
1323

Jules Bastien-Lepage often painted the peasants of his hometown of Damvillers in northeastern France. Here the 'little wild girl' of the title patiently and quietly guards a cow. The artist makes the girl seem isolated, alone in the barren, winter landscape – she is dwarfed by the tall thistle and the leafless tree. There is also a feeling of sadness from her haunting eyes and the way she pulls her rags around her as if for warmth. (When D.H. Lawrence saw this painting in London in 1909 he said that 'the little pinched face looking out of the sack haunts me and terrifies me and reproaches me.') Bastien-Lepage often exhibited his paintings in Britain, where they were both popular and successful. The Glasgow Boys copied Bastien-Lepage's subjects, his broad blocky brushstrokes and even the way he signed his name.

EVERY PICTURE TELLS A STORY

In this interactive gallery you can explore objects to discover the stories behind them. Each exhibit shows there is often more to a painting or artefact than first meets the eye. The fascinating exhibits range from Victorian paintings that reveal tales of times long ago to a Maori boat stern, where the elaborate carvings tell of the creation legend. Other objects of Burmese and Islamic origin prove that storytelling is a universal phenomenon, taking place across cultures and time. Amongst other things, the humorous interactive elements allow you to help characters decide their fate or choose an ending to a story!

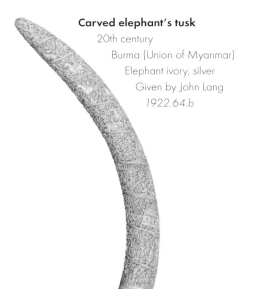

Carved elephant's tusk
20th century
Burma (Union of Myanmar)
Elephant ivory, silver
Given by John Lang
1922.64.b

This elephant's tusk with its embossed silver mount is carved with detailed scenes from a story from one of the lives of the Buddha. It tells of the demon Punnaka and the sage Vidhura, an incarnation of the Buddha. It is taken from one of the 550 Jataka tales that illustrate the Buddha's path to enlightenment and is called the Vidhura-Pandita Jataka. Burmese ivory carving began in the 1860s in the court of King Mindon in Mandalay. Larger carvings of whole tusks became common in the late nineteenth and early twentieth centuries. Most of these carvings had a spiritual theme — wealthy patrons paid for the ivory and donated the finished piece to a temple as a good deed.

La Faruk Madonna
1941–42
Giuseppe Baldan
(1905–74)
Oils on the reverse of
flour bags
PP.1995.16.a

This is one of a set of remarkable paintings done on the reverse of old flour bags by Italian prisoner of war Giuseppe Baldan and which formed the altarpiece of a simple mud chapel erected in a prisoner of war camp in what is now Somalia. The camp was set up by the British during World War II, and held mostly Italian prisoners. The artist chose to paint the Virgin and Child adored by two angels against the background of the actual camp, creating a unique visual record. It includes the field hospital, cemetery and even the mud chapel. The paintings were saved from destruction when the camp was disbanded and given to Captain Alfred Hawksworth, the camp commander. He was encouraged to keep them by the Italian prisoners of war in gratitude for his fair and humane treatment of all prisoners who passed through the camp.

**Two Strings to Her
Bow** c.1887
John Pettie
(1839–93)
Oil on canvas
826 x 1194 mm
Given by Sir John
Muir, 1888
663

The Victorians
loved anecdotes,
or pictures that
told a story, and
Pettie's pictures were
extremely popular
because of their
frivolous or light-
hearted nature. His
work was almost
always historical or
literary in content, so
although this picture
was painted in 1887,
the three central
characters wear
Regency costumes
dating from around
1815–20. Its great
appeal lies in the
contented expression
on the girl's face.
She is perfectly
happy with two
suitors attending her,
although each of
them clearly wishes
their rival would
disappear!

Islamic shield, 19th century, Iran or India (Deccan)
Steel inlaid with silver and brass using the bidri
technique
A.1952.48.h

This shield shows the Prophet Muhammad in the form of a
gazelle and his cousin Imam Ali Ibn-Abi-Talib in the form of a
lion. The gazelle represents the perfect beauty of the Islamic
faith (the Prophet being the ideal Muslim), protected by the
lion, the warrior of the faith, led by Imam Ali, famous for his
legendary strength and fearlessness.

It was probably made for a Muslim belonging to
the Shi'a sect of Islam, a member of the ruling classes in
nineteenth-century Mughal India, and could have been used
in Ashura ceremonies. The shapes of the gazelle and lion
are made from Arabic calligraphic script – the script forming
the gazelle on the right and its mirror image on the left is
from 'The Gulistan' (The Rose Garden), a poem composed
by the Iranian Sufi mystic Sa'di in 1258. This particular verse
describes the qualities of the Prophet Muhammad. The script
that shapes the lion is a talismanic prayer to Ali.

SCOTTISH IDENTITY IN ART

Many of the things we associate with Scotland have been captured and communicated in art. The displays in this gallery examine where ideas of 'Scottishness' came from – rugged landscapes, stags at bay, tartan – but some contemporary images are also included to illustrate that many of these are still linked with Scottish identity today.

The art of any particular period is complemented by objects from Scotland's material culture, things which have uniquely Scottish characteristics, design or decoration, reinforcing our distinctiveness as a nation. Images of famous Scots such as William Wallace, Mary, Queen of Scots and Robert Burns come under scrutiny, and an entertaining video interactive allows Scots of today to have their say!

The Massacre of Glencoe, 1883–86
James Hamilton (1853–94)
Oil on canvas
1067 x 1829 mm
Given by the family of D. Brodie MacLeod, 1929
1790

Scottish painter James Hamilton depicts the massacre of Glencoe of 1692 in this oil painting. He shows survivors who escaped the treacherous attack on them by government forces. Hiding in the hills, and safe from the troops, this small group of men, women and children now faces terrible weather conditions without any shelter as they watch their homes burn in the valley below. This massacre inflamed Highland resistance to the British government. Hamilton indicates this by showing armed clansmen nearby the refugees, as if ready to defend people and property.

Scroll-butt pistol c.1715, Scottish, made by Patrick Buchanan of Glasgow, steel, silver, 350 x 150 mm
Bought with grant aid from the Art Fund and the National Fund for Acquisitions, 1978
A.1978.29

This flintlock pistol is one of only three Glasgow-made pistols known to exist, as most of the surviving early Scottish firearms were made in the east coast burghs that dominated production. Often many of the more delicate parts are lost from pistols, but this one is perfectly preserved with all its original features. Its all-metal construction and scroll-butt are distinctively Scottish, but it is larger than others in the collection. Vibrantly decorated, both the engraving and silver inlay are accentuated with punched dots. The butt and trigger are offset to suit a right-handed marksman. Strangely, the Glasgow maker misspelled his name as 'Buhanan' when he signed it!

Heroism and Humanity c.1840
William Allan
(1782–1850)
Oil on canvas
1270 x 1969 mm
Given by William S. Steel, 1909
1233

William Allan was a famous Scottish history painter. Here he has painted a scene from King Robert the Bruce's life. The King is shown in a yellow coat decorated with the lion of Scotland, imploring others to protect an abandoned family and a priest. Thankfully, kinsman Edward Bruce and some soldiers are at hand to obey the King's command. Like his friend Sir Walter Scott, Allan creates a romantic vision of Scottish history where monarchy and church protect ordinary people – supporting the painting's title and theme.

Mr and Mrs Robert N. Campbell of Kailzie c.1800–6
Henry Raeburn (1756–1823)
Oil on canvas
2413 x 1524 mm
Bequeathed by Isabella A.H.J. Campbell, 1915
1594

Mr and Mrs Campbell stroll romantically in the grounds of their estate of Kailzie at Traquair, Peebles-shire, and are captured as if the artist has just met them. In reality, the highly fashionable couple were probably painted in Raeburn's Edinburgh studio, with the surroundings added separately. Raeburn's talent lay in his ability to catch character with just a few strokes of paint, and he was such a master of reflected light that this picture is totally convincing. Often praised as his country's best painter, his period of activity ran parallel with Scotland's golden age of scientific discovery, invention and learning – the Enlightenment.

The Last of the Clan 1865
Thomas Faed (1826–1900)
Oil on canvas
1448 x 1829 mm
Bought by Glasgow Museums
with the aid of the Heritage
Grant for Scotland, the Art
Fund, the Pilgrim Trust and
public subscription, 1980
3366

The Highland Clearances are
remembered as a shameful
time. Many Scots were forced
to emigrate, driven from their
land by poverty, or evicted by
greedy estate owners. Thomas
Faed exhibited this painting at
the Royal Academy in 1865.
Although by then the worst of
the Clearances were over, the
story told by the picture still
aroused strong feelings and
inspired him to create the most
enduring image of this tragic
period of Scottish history.

Grief is written on the faces
of young and old, and even
the horse, as the unseen ship
sails away. There is beauty,
however, in the skilfully painted
young women, surely out of
place in their London fashions,
and random objects scattered
on the quayside.

**Gentleman's tartan
coat** c.1820–30
Wool
850 x 550 mm
Given by
Dr Elizabeth
Alexander,
1938
E.1938.92.a

This coat of hard (stiff) tartan was woven
using vibrant green and red wools. When
it was given to Glasgow Museums in
1938 it was said to have belonged to
Bonnie Prince Charlie. However, its cut
– with the double-breasted front, bias
(diagonal) cut cloth and cut-away tails –
dates from the reign of George IV.
When the King visited Edinburgh in 1822,
Sir Walter Scott, who was involved in
organizing the celebrations, called for
everyone to wear tartan. George IV is said
to have teamed his kilt with flesh-coloured
stockings, but more fashionable men wore
fitted coats of tartan such as this example.

**Christ of St John of the
Cross** 1951
Salvador Dalí (1904–89)
Oil on canvas
2048 x 1159 mm
Bought by Glasgow
Museums, 1952
2964

Kelvingrove's most famous
picture is one of the most
striking religious images of the
twentieth century. Depicting
the central theme of the
Christian faith – the death of
Jesus Christ on the cross, Dalí
shows Him 'as beautiful as
the God that He is', without
any contortion or agony. The
usual crown of thorns and
nails through His hands and
feet are not there. Instead,
the dramatic light bathes the
fine muscles of this strong,
young man. The daring angle
of His body was inspired by
a drawing Dalí saw by the
sixteenth-century Spanish
Carmelite friar, St John of the
Cross.

GLASGOW'S INTERNATIONAL EXHIBITIONS

Glasgow's International Exhibitions of 1888 and 1901 followed in the fashion set by the Great Exhibition of 1851 in London. These big ambitious projects were a celebration of late Victorian Glasgow – its industry, art and culture, trade and commerce. They were meant to show off the city in a positive way to the rest of the world, and to reflect Glasgow's world links. When Queen Victoria visited the 1888 Exhibition, it was a triumph.

The objects on display are chosen to give a flavour of the Exhibitions, the serious and fun sides, what people saw when they visited, and the souvenirs they kept.

Objects from the Indian Courts, the Great Exhibition 1888

The Indian and Ceylon Courts helped give the 1888 Glasgow International Exhibition its international element. Three huge courts were filled with products and produce from India, Pakistan and Bangladesh, with a separate court for Sri Lanka. John Muir, of Glasgow company James Finlay & Co., chaired the Indian Committee, which organized this section of the exhibition.

T.N. Mukharji of the Indian Museum, Calcutta, advised on a list of 'art manufactures' (sic) for the Indian courts. He brought together a wide range of quality craft ware, including jewellery, textiles and metalware. A delicate and intricate rosewater sprinkler in the shape of a crane was probably sourced from Dhaka, Bangladesh. The carved and lacquered bed, or *charpoi*, legs came from Rajastan. The art of damascening, a skilled method of working with precious metals, is seen in caskets from Sialkot, Pakistan and the elaborate tray from Kerala. The bidri ware water bottle and stopper is a fine example of this specialized form of metalwork.

From Sri Lanka, the Tea Planters Association in Colombo organized displays in the Ceylon Court, including the two brass dishes in the case. After the exhibition closed Glasgow Museums bought, or was given, many of the objects that had been on display.

Rosewater sprinkler with crane holding a fish in its beak
1888
Probably Dhaka, Bangladesh
Silver
360 x 60 mm
1888.109.gi

Dish with peacocks and tigers 1888
Sri Lanka
Beaten brass, 360 mm
1888.105.f

Lipton silver
Model frigate trophy 1901
Silver, 1020 x 900 x 260 mm
Given by Thomas Lipton,
1932
1932.29.bo

In 1932, Glasgow received a bequest from one of its favourite sons, Sir Thomas Lipton (1850–1931), of a large sum of money to benefit the poor of the city, along with his volumes of press cuttings, *objets de vertu*, medals of honour and his amazing collection of trophies. The *objets de vertu* are mainly formal gifts, and the medals include honours from Serbia and Italy in recognition of his humanitarian war work. Most of the trophies are yachting prizes, won by Lipton on his 'Shamrock' yachts in Scotland, England, Germany and the USA. Others were presented by employees or by his peers, including the casket by Edward & Sons, Glasgow, which held the scroll awarding him the freedom of the city in 1923. One of the most unusual trophies is a *nef* in the shape of a masted sailing ship. It was won in 1901 by Lipton's yacht *Shamrock* at the International Race for First Class Yachts. Undoubtedly the most splendid of the trophies is by Tiffany of New York. This was presented in 1930 to Lipton, 'the Gamest Loser in the World of Sport', by the American people to demonstrate their affection and respect for him when he failed, despite five attempts, to win the Americas' Cup.

Working model of the steam engine from SS *Buenos Aires* 1887
David Carlaw, William Denny Brothers
Wood, metal, brass, 980 x 850 x 610 mm
T.1962.10

Glasgow scientific instrument and model maker David Carlaw made this working model of a quadruple expansion marine steam engine. It was shown at the Glasgow International Exhibition in 1888 and was described as 'the most beautiful engine model ever produced'. Walter Brock designed the quadruple expansion engine to get as much power from steam as possible by passing it through four cylinders in turn. These engines cost more to build, but were much more fuel-efficient than other steam engines. The full-size engine was used in SS *Buenos Aires*, built by Denny's of Dumbarton for the new Spanish government mail contract to Buenos Aires, Argentina. She was launched in August 1887 and broken up in 1942.

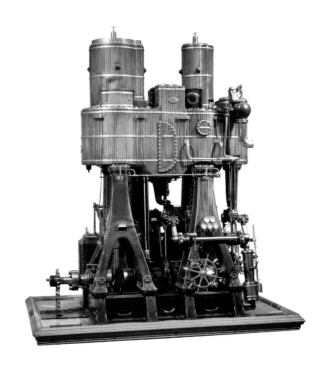

SCOTLAND'S FIRST PEOPLE

The Scotland's First People gallery invites you to take a trip into the distant past, from the first evidence of humans in Scotland through to the time of the Vikings. The diverse collection of artefacts – including carved stone balls, cup-and-ring-marked stone, cist slabs, excavated materials, domestic objects and weaponry – provides a vivid window into life in Mesolithic and Neolithic times, as well as into death and ritual practices in the Bronze Age, early medieval water settlements, and the peaceful and violent aspects of Viking life in Scotland.

Axehead
1600–1500 BC
Bronze, 98 x 69 mm
Given by David Patrick, 1959
A.1959.20.c

Axehead
1600–1500 BC
Bronze
125 x 25 mm
Given by David Patrick, 1959
A.1959.20.b

Dagger
1600–1500 BC
Bronze
258 x 67 mm
Given by David Patrick, 1959
A.1959.20.a

The Gavel Moss Hoard

These ancient weapons – the blade of a dagger and two axeheads – are from the Bronze Age, and are thought to be at least 3,500 years old. They were found in 1790 by a farmer when he was ploughing his field at Gavel Moss Farm near Lochwinnoch, southwest of Glasgow.

The Gavel Moss weapons are of exceptional quality. The dagger has three ridges that converge just before the point. As well as creating the illusion of a curved weapon, this ridge design served to strengthen the dagger, which would have originally had a grip of wood or horn riveted into the holes at the base of the blade. One axe has cable ornament running down its sides, while the sides of the smaller axe are decorated with a chevron pattern.

Why would such fine examples of undamaged weaponry have been buried in the ground? They could have been placed there as an offering to the gods. Or possibly a desperate person buried the hoard as a means of safekeeping in a time of great danger, but was never able to retrieve them. The farmer, Mr Latta, gave the hoard to his niece on her marriage into the Patrick family in 1810. David Patrick donated the objects to Glasgow Museums in 1959.

Carved stone ball 3300–2000 BC
Alford, 70 x 70 x 70 mm
Bequeathed by Ludovic McLellan Mann, 1955
A.1955.96.sq

This is one of three small and extremely intriguing finds dating to the Neolithic or Early Bronze Age. Over 425 carved stone balls have been found in Scotland, mostly in Aberdeenshire. As suggested by the three on display in Kelvingrove, the decoration on carved balls varies greatly – many have protruding shapes, others incised spirals, circles, cross hatchings or lines.

Two of the balls on display in the museum were donated by Ludovic McLellan Mann (1869–1955), an eminent and controversial archaeologist who was active in the early twentieth century. Because most of the carved balls that have been found are the same size, Mann argued that they were used as weights. Other people have speculated that the stones were used as weapons – as projectiles fired at enemies from some sort of sling – or even for games. But the absence of chipping on the surface of the balls conflicts with these suggestions. It is more likely, given their detailed decoration, that they were highly prized objects, used as status symbols or to bring good fortune.

Satchel probably 6th to 9th century
Leather
350 x 350 x 200 mm
A.1960.46.dy

These remains of an early medieval satchel are the oldest ever found in Scotland, and were discovered during the excavation of the artificial island settlement at Loch Glashan in the 1960s. The different leather panels that formed the satchel were preserved by the waterlogged conditions of the site. The satchel would have been held together and decorated with leather thongs, and the holes for these can still be seen. Early pictures show monks carrying bags similar to this satchel, indicating that it would probably have held a religious book, annals or possibly the relics of saints.

Artist's impression of how the satchel may have looked.

Log boat probably 1st to 10th century
Oak, 3060 x 860 x 780 mm
A.1961.37.a

This log boat was discovered in 1960 in Loch Glashan, Argyll. Carved from a single piece of oak, the boat has one seat and a hole in the bow for attaching a length of rope. The dimensions of the boat suggest that it would have been ideally suited for taking people around the loch, providing an efficient means of transport. The boat is now very fragile due to the great age of the wood.

CONFLICT AND CONSEQUENCE

Human conflict and its consequences are explored in this gallery. The equipment and fighting techniques of warriors from different places, times and social groups are examined. Among the wide range of objects exhibited are magnificent medieval and Renaissance armours, early firearms and traditional Scottish weapons. Some of the arms and armour belonged to people of the highest rank, and this is reflected in the quality and decoration. Many of these weapons are beautiful and skilfully created while being potentially lethal at the same time. Other displays tell the stories of ordinary soldiers, or civilians caught up in warfare.

Armour of the First Earl of Pembroke c.1557
Made by Erasmus Kirkener, Greenwich
Steel, copper alloy, leather, gold
1900 x 850 x 500 mm
E.1939.65.a.1

Reinforcing breastplate or plackart 1557
Made by Erasmus Kirkener, Greenwich
Steel and gold
460 x 305 x 180 mm
Bought with grant aid from the Art Fund, the Heritage Lottery Fund and the Friends of Glasgow Museums, 2004
A.2004.8

The armour created for Sir William Herbert, the first Earl of Pembroke, around 1557 is the finest of its time made by the Royal Workshop at Greenwich. This workshop, first created by King Henry VIII of England, produced armour for the leading courtiers and nobles of the realm.

This armour is the only one from Greenwich to survive with its complete matching horse armour. Sir William may have ordered it specially for leading an army on the continent. The armour has many exchange pieces, such as a reinforcing breastplate or plackart. These allowed the armour to be used in different combinations to suit different kinds of fighting – whether Sir William was in battle as a light, medium or heavy cavalryman or on foot.

The armour is very finely made. Not only is it carefully shaped to fit, but is also decorated with etched and gilt strap-work to proclaim the high status of its owner. Although the armour is now brown, it would originally have been bright steel polished to a shining finish. No one on the battlefield would have been in any doubt about the importance of the wearer.

Marianne Grant Holocaust artworks collection

Children playing in winter with hot ashes from the stoves that heated the dwellings 1943, Marianne Grant (1921–2007), Pencil, paper
Bought with grant aid from the Heritage Lottery Fund, the Art Fund and the
National Fund for Acquisitions, 2004
PP.2005.38.1–77

Marianne Grant's art helped her to stay alive during the Holocaust. She was born in Prague to Jewish parents, and loved to paint and draw. In 1942, when she and her mother were deported to the Theresienstadt ghetto, Marianne packed watercolours, brushes and paper in the suitcase she was allowed to bring.

When Marianne's mother was sent to Auschwitz, Marianne jumped on to the train to be with her. In Auschwitz Marianne came to the attention of Dr Mengele, who used prisoners for horrific medical experiments. She was required to use her artistic skills for Dr Mengele, who gave her an architect's drawing kit. While she was working, Mengele paced up and down and Marianne knew that if she made a mistake she would be finished – she was drawing for her life.

In April 1945, Marianne and her mother were sent to Bergen-Belsen concentration camp. After the liberation of the camp by the British army, they went to Sweden where Marianne earned a living by making Christmas decorations. Throughout the war Marianne painted and sketched the scenes she saw around her. In 1951 she married and came to live and raise a family in Glasgow. This painting shows children playing in the ashes at Theresienstadt, and is signed 'MH 19.11.43 Terezin. Deti u popela [children at the ashes]'.

Ura (The Exile) 1926
Benno Schotz
Mahogany bust
400 x 355 x 228 mm
Bought by Glasgow
Museums, 1929
S.183

Ura Collins and Benno Schotz, both Jewish immigrants to Scotland, became close for a while. Ura inspired her friend to carve this elegant portrait of her, which gains drama from the energetic turn of the head. Restless and idealistic, Ura left Scotland for excitement and political activity in Paris. She escaped the Nazis during World War II, when she was shielded by a brave French family. Ura then sought a new life in the Soviet Union, only to be sent into internal exile and never heard of again. Her life story, as told by a relative who still lives in Glasgow, is a poignant part of the display Remembering for the Future.

HISTORY DISCOVERY CENTRE

Here you will find interactives and objects that you can handle to discover how people lived at various times in the past. Particularly poignant is the story of the short life of Margaret Hutchison, but you can also find out about people who lived during the Bronze Age; experience what it was like living in Ancient Egypt; understand what life was like in the Victorian era; discover how the Chimu people lived in Peru hundreds of years ago; learn about Highland life in Scotland during the 1700s – and find out what teenagers in Glasgow think will happen to the objects they leave behind and what they might tell future generations about life in Glasgow today.

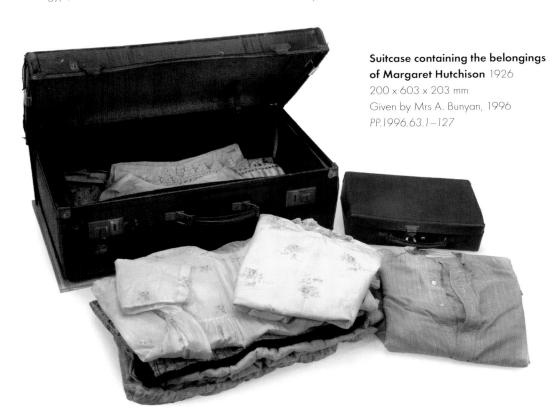

**Suitcase containing the belongings
of Margaret Hutchison** 1926
*200 x 603 x 203 mm
Given by Mrs A. Bunyan, 1996
PP.1996.63.1–127*

Margaret Hutchison's life is told through her belongings, which fitted into one suitcase. She was born at home in Burnhouse Street, Maryhill, Glasgow, at 5.20am on 25 July 1918. She died aged seven years and six months on Hogmanay 1925/26, after failing to come out of an anaesthetic in hospital. She was buried on 4 January, and the funeral cost £10 and 8 shillings.

What do we know about Margaret? She was small with a dark bob, and liked cats. She collected scraps, hankies, purses and small treasures. She played shops in the backcourt of her tenement home with little bits of broken pottery for coins. She had a skipping rope, and was knitting with yellow and beige wool. She went to Sunday School and had an invitation to the Christmas party. She loved her Granny, whose picture she kept in an old cigar box. Margaret had tackety boots, shoes and a pair of worn slippers, a smart velvet coat and a few homemade day dresses, a school jumper and bloomers and nightdresses. After Margaret died her mother packed all her personal belongings into a suitcase, which was kept in the family for 70 years.

CULTURAL SURVIVAL

This gallery is about different cultures and their survival. It explores the idea that some cultures may have been lost, but many more have adapted to influences from outside and survived. The displays Last Pearl Fisherman of Scotland and St Kilda: On the Edge of the World are about Scottish cultures. Survival: People and Their Land, Kingdom of Africa: Benin, and Ceremonial Turtle Posts look at cultures in other parts of the world. In these displays we are trying to show that people have to adapt in order to survive, that societies throughout the world are very diverse, and finally, that the environment is a major influence on the survival of human cultures. Each of the five displays takes up one or more of these key messages of survival.

Six 2 Six shield 1980s
Wahgi, Mt Hagen, Papua New Guinea
Wood and cane
1620 x 500 x 130 mm
Bought with assistance from the National Fund for Acquisitions
A.2003.4

Buka War 1990
Mathias Kauage
(1944–2003)
Acrylic on canvas
1250 x 1755 mm
Bought by Glasgow Museums, 1994
3546

For over a decade, the island of Bougainville and its neighbour Buka in Papua New Guinea became the site of a civil war which grew out of opposition to the Panguna mine, one of the world's largest gold and copper mines. The long conflict was a frequent subject for Mathias Kauage and other Papua New Guinean artists. The graphic images in their narrative paintings acted as a running commentary on the war. This work illustrates an incident when the indigenous Bougainville Revolutionary Army stole explosives and used them to destroy installations at the mine, which led to its closure in 1988. The letters CRT on the bulldozer are the initials of Conzinc Rio Tinto, the mining company.

This battle shield was used in the late 1980s by the Senglap people from the Wahgi area of Highland Papua New Guinea in a dispute with their neighbours, the Dange, following a road accident. All shields carried by the group involved in the warfare were painted by Kaipel Ka, a local sign writer. Most are decorated with the phrase 'Six 2 Six', normally referring to an all-night party, but in this case indicating that the group can fight all day. In recent years inter-group warfare amongst the Wahgi people has increased. Wooden shields such as this one are used in areas where guns are forbidden.

CULTURAL SURVIVAL

Zogo baur, ceremonial post 19th century
Dauar Island, Torres Strait, Australia
Wood, human bone, shell
3330 x 160 x 70 mm
Given by Robert Bruce
1889.67.bh.1

One of a pair, this male ceremonial post with the carved turtle at its base was once painted with ochre and decorated with shell ornaments. It was part of a traditional celebration of the fertility of people and nature on Dauar Island in the Torres Strait between Australia and Papua New Guinea. The posts were found in a cave by Robert Bruce, a Scottish missionary who took them back to Glasgow in 1889. They may have been hidden when the islanders converted to Christianity in 1871 and stopped openly practising their traditions. In spite of this, much of Torres Strait Islanders' traditional culture has survived, and the posts retain their spiritual importance to the communities. There have been no formal requests for the posts to be returned to their original home but in accordance with the islanders' wishes, their story is being told in Kelvingrove.

Pot of Life 2005
Lucky Oboh and Ikpomwosa Inneh
Benin City, Nigeria, Africa
Brass, lead
Commissioned by Glasgow Museums, 2005
A.2006.1.a–c

Made in 2005, the *Pot of Life* is the first contemporary Benin 'bronze' commissioned for a British museum. Traditional West African techniques of lost wax casting dating to at least the sixteenth century were used to make this intriguing work of art. In Edo mythology those who search for, and find, the pot of life are able to visit the spirit world where they right injustice and encounter a range of beings before returning to the physical world.

Lucky Oboh's contemporary *Pot of Life* is an innovative design based on a nineteenth-century bronze from Benin City. The lidded bowl decorated with wild animals and sacred regalia sits on a stand composed of two snakes and a base with a further tableau of wild creatures. It is an imaginative exploration of a forest where powerful beings inhabit the borders between the physical and spiritual worlds.

St Kilda

For historical reasons, Glasgow has strong links with the Western Highlands and Islands, and our collections reflect this. Material from St Kilda, until 1930 the remotest inhabited island group in the British Isles, includes both natural history and domestic objects. Although uninhabited now, except by scientists, the islands of St Kilda provide rich material for study.

St Kilda field mouse

Apodemus sylvaticus hirtensis
1982
Freeze-dried skin
110 x 210 x 220 mm
Z.1982.60.2

Soay sheep *Ovis aries adult male*
1980
Mounted skin, 850 x 830 x 480 mm
DB.3415

Soay sheep and the St Kilda mice

Because of their remote position, 64 kilometres west of Harris in the Outer Hebrides, the islands of St Kilda are very important for wildlife. The islands support the largest breeding colony of northern gannets in the world, with over 60,000 pairs and some of the largest colonies of fulmar, puffin and other seabirds in Britain.

The islands are also home for some very special and unique mammals. The island of Soay is the original home of the Soay sheep, the most primitive form of domestic sheep in Europe. They may have been taken there about 4,000 years ago by the first inhabitants of

the islands. Some were moved to the main island, Hirta, in 1932, and this flock has been intensely studied by scientists since 1955. Sheep numbers build up over a few years, only to crash again when the limited vegetation on the islands cannot support the large population in a hard winter.

Two kinds of mice used to occur on St Kilda, both larger forms of mainland species. The St Kilda house mouse, which fed mainly on grain and other human commodities, became extinct shortly after people left the islands in 1930. The St Kilda field mouse is still common on Hirta.

St Kilda mailboat
Wood, lead, twine and skin
240 x 700 x 280 mm
A.1967.9.a

These little wooden boats held a letter and postage sealed in a cocoa tin, and were used by the isolated islanders of St Kilda to communicate with people on the mainland. Before a steamer service started in 1877, bringing summer tourists and a new source of income, there was no regular contact with the mainland — these mailboats were the only method of communication. Islanders placed their letters, with money to pay for stamps, inside the mailboats and then set them into the sea to float to the mainland and — hopefully — into the hands of a benevolent person who would then post the letter.

STUDY CENTRE

The Study Centre is full of information to help you find out more about the collections on display. Here you can investigate objects, talk to staff, use the online resources, or sit and browse through the reference books in the Reading Room. There are also displays in the Study Centre and pictured in this section are some of the objects currently on view.

You can bring in your own objects to the Study Centre, either for staff to identify them, or for you to carry out your own research. Please note that we are unable to give valuations.

Glasgow's silver

Early silver made and marked in Glasgow is very rare, and the pieces in our collection date from the later seventeenth century until today. They served many purposes – domestic, ecclesiastical, civic, regimental, commemorative and presentation.

The earliest known example of Glasgow domestic silver is Thomas Moncur II's small tumbler cup of about 1680. Some pieces – the quaichs and thistle mugs – are distinctively Scottish, while continental European influences are seen in some earlier pieces, such as William Clerk's patch box (c.1695), and John Luke's large 1704 quaich. By the 1730s, the coffee, tea and chocolate pots, salvers and waiters, wine funnels, tea caddies, sugar bowls and cutlery revealed the influence of fashionable London designs, such as the impressive rococo tea kettle by James Glen (c.1750). The neoclassical goblet by Adam Graham (c.1780), made from silver mined in Islay, is an important historical document. Robert Gray's fine work dominated the Glasgow silver trade during the first decades of the nineteenth century. The Art Nouveau 1902 Edinburgh Gold Cup by D.C. Rait shows the quality achieved by twentieth-century Glasgow silversmiths.

The Glasgow Assay Office was established in 1819 and its 1964 closure is commemorated by an Edward & Sons bowl – the last silver to have the distinctive 'tree, bell, fish and ring' Glasgow hallmark. Recent work confirms the continuing strength of the art and craft of the silversmith in Glasgow, and includes work by John Creed and prize-winning entries by students of the Glasgow School of Art for the Young Designer Silversmith of the Year Award.

Fish slice 1822
Made by Robert Gray & Son
Silver
31 x 62 mm
Bought by Glasgow Museums
E.1979.58

Quaich 1704
Made by John Luke Jr
Silver
Bought with grant aid from the National Fund
for Acquisitions and the Art Fund, 1984
E.1983.30

Sugar nippers c.1750
Made by William Shaw, London
Silver
15 x 52 mm
Given by Victor J. Cumming, 1946
E.1946.87.cy

The Hull Grundy collection

From 1976 until her death in 1984, Mrs Anne Hull Grundy gifted a large collection of historic jewellery to Glasgow Museums. Mrs Hull Grundy was an important twentieth-century collector who believed passionately that the significance of jewellery is greatly under-estimated. She talked of how jewellery mirrors the world it comes from in miniature, how it highlights changing tastes, fashionable obsessions and interests, technical and manufacturing developments, economic and social history.

The majority of the earrings, rings, brooches, bracelets and bangles, waist buckles and belts, buttons, shoe buckles, hair ornaments, necklaces and necklets in the gift are English-made. Some are from continental Europe, mainly France. Most date from the nineteenth century, with some pieces from the late eighteenth and early twentieth centuries. Sentimental jewellery, such as tokens of love, remembrance or of mourning, predominates. Themes include the natural world – animals, plants and flowers; faraway places and cultures; historical periods and nineteenth-century 'novelties'; jewellery which referenced contemporary life. Mrs Hull Grundy made gifts to numerous museums throughout the United Kingdom, and selected pieces to ensure the collections were suited to the area each museum served. She created two groups especially for Glasgow – nineteenth-century 'Scottish pebblestone' jewellery and Art Nouveau pieces from the turn of the nineteenth and twentieth centuries.

Modern Ghost Dance shirt 1998, Lakota, South Dakota
Undyed cotton, feathers, natural pigments, buffalo hide
Given by Marcella LeBeau, Wounded Knee Survivors' Association, 1998
A.1998.9

In early 1892, Glasgow Museums acquired a Ghost Dance shirt from the Lakota interpreter at Buffalo Bill's Wild West Show in Dennistoun. The shirt was said to be 'taken from Sioux Warrior killed at the Battle of Wounded Knee'. Its association with Wounded Knee makes it sacred to the Lakota people. In 1992, the shirt was on display in Glasgow when it was seen by an American lawyer who contacted some of the Lakota.

This shirt is a replica of that original Ghost Dance shirt, which was given back to the Lakota people of South Dakota by Glasgow City Council in 1999. The replica was formally presented to Glasgow at a public hearing in November 1998, attended by the Lakota descendents of survivors of the massacre at Wounded Knee in December 1890. The modern shirt was made by Marcella LeBeau, a descendent of Rain in the Face, a Lakota warrior who survived the massacre. She decorated it with a buffalo hide strip and red clay from the Cheyenne River Reservation and ring-necked pheasant feathers.

Serpent brooch late 18th–early 19th century
Gold, enamel, glass, human hair
36 x 32 x 9 mm
Given by Mrs Hull Grundy, 1976
E.1976.1.764

Mourning pendant c.1807
Gold, enamel, glass, human hair
41 x 27 x 5 mm
Given by Mrs Hull Grundy, 1976
E.1976.1.765

The Centre of New Enlightenment

The Centre of New Enlightenment (TCoNE) is an inspiring educational experience and adventure. Created in collaboration with Sir Tom Hunter's Hunter Foundation, this world-class attraction is the latest addition to the innovative Campbell Hunter Education Wing.

Visitors are escorted to the mysterious TCoNE Central Technical Area where they are briefed and issued with unique specialist equipment. Kit includes a state-of-the-art PDA (a hand-held computer), the coolest computers in town. The PDAs issue challenges to visitors, who explore the galleries in pairs, solving clues and completing challenges. Visitors' results are compiled and put on a special website that celebrates our achievements.

A cornerstone of the Scottish Curriculum for Excellence is to enable young people to become confident individuals. The TCoNE programme has been designed so that visitors will discover their own character strengths and build self-confidence through encounters with objects in Kelvingrove. Plus it's really good fun!

Why enlightenment? A long time ago, people in Scotland started to question accepted ideas. They looked around and thought, 'Does the world have to be this way?' This was the beginning of the Enlightenment in Scotland. They changed their world into the one we see today. Now it is our turn to change the future. The Centre of New Enlightenment is the place to start.

Museum Services

Glasgow Museums has 1.4 million objects in store, as well as archive, library and photographic resources. We welcome research on our collections, and appointments can be made to view objects or to talk to staff members.

You can find out more about objects in the Kelvingrove Study Centre (see p.66) but you may also like to visit Glasgow Museums Resource Centre, a purpose-built publicly accessible museum storage facility in the south of the city. There you can book guided tours of the stores, join in our programme of workshops and activities, or consult Collections Navigator, an online database of our collections (accessible from all our venues). Using this you can order objects for individual or group study in our dedicated object study rooms. There is also a reference library and archive facility. Visit www.glasgowmuseums.com for further information.

Exhibitions and Events Kelvingrove has a changing programme of temporary exhibitions and displays. In the Community Exhibition space you can find out more about the work of some of our partners. A regular programme of events takes place throughout the year.

Visitor Facilities Kelvingrove has a restaurant and café, as well as shops stocking a range of gifts and souvenirs. Our Photo Library offers a range of services, including a bespoke print service. Tours of the galleries are available (see below), but please contact us in advance. Kelvingrove Art Gallery and Museum is also available to hire for functions big or small.

Volunteer Guides Our knowledgeable and experienced volunteer guides offer free tours of Kelvingrove, and can provide tours for visitors with a visual impairment or in different languages if booked in advance.

Learning & Access Glasgow Museums has a large Learning & Access team who provide a wide variety of services, from addressing difficult social issues in high profile citywide projects to running fun, creative and social events for families and other visitors in all our venues.

The Open Museum outreach service works with communities across the city, facilitating access to collections through reminiscence and handling kits, travelling exhibitions, community-based exhibitions and project work. The team also develops and supports community participation through permanent community museums and exhibition spaces. Learning & Access and the Museums Education Service offer learning opportunities through a programme for pre-5s, primary and secondary pupils (led or self-led) and CPD for teachers. The Volunteer Service supports opportunities for people of all ages to get involved with museums, using existing skills and developing new ones, along with social integration, and job training.

Friends of Glasgow Museums (FoGM) One of the longest established friends organizations in the UK, the association supports the work of Glasgow Museums and fosters interest in the arts in Glasgow. Through membership and fund-raising activities, FoGM contributes many thousands of pounds each year to Glasgow Museums to buy and/or conserve works of art and other objects, and to support the provision of other services. A regular programme of excursions, trips and lectures is one of the benefits of membership, and new members are always welcome. For full details of all our facilities, and for contact information, please visit www.glasgowmuseums.com.

Supporting us Glasgow Museums is part of Culture and Sport Glasgow (CSG), which was established in April 2007. CSG operates as a charity, and part of its remit is to deliver cultural services for the city of Glasgow. All of Glasgow's museums and libraries continue to offer free entry to the people of Glasgow and visitors to the city.

During your visit today you will have seen donation boxes in Kelvingrove. As part of a commitment to fundraising, CSG aims to revive the 'Culture of Giving' with the introduction of donation boxes throughout museum and key library venues. This form of fundraising helps us to provide an even better service than we could otherwise afford. Since the boxes were introduced, we are on track to reach our target of £250,000 for 2009/10 at the time of writing. We have also introduced Gift Aid forms and envelopes, which allow us to claim back tax on all qualifying donations. In practice, this means that for every £1 you give with a completed Gift Aid declaration, we actually receive £1.28. We are also delighted to receive donations from our overseas visitors, although Gift Aid does not apply to those. (Further information can be found at http://www.hmrc.gov.uk/charities/gift-aid.htm)

Thank you for your support.

Index <small>Italics denote illustrations</small>